DO YOU KNOW GOD'S HOLY SABBATHS, FEASTS, AND LAWS?

Make the
Connection

LANCE CASWELL

*I gratefully acknowledge the generosity of
FreeBibleImages.com
in allowing me to use their images
in this book.*

*Map of the Twelve Tribes of Israel
From Wikimedia Commons, the free media repository*

DEDICATION

This book is dedicated to all who diligently seek the truth and are delighted in the knowledge and application of the truth.

DO YOU KNOW GOD'S HOLY SABBATHS, FEASTS, AND LAWS?

Make the Connection

by Lance Caswell

First Edition • Copyright © 2016

ISBN: 978-0-9978100-0-4

Page Layout | Arrow Computer Services

Printed and Bound in the United States

For more information, visit Lance Caswell online at:
www.lancecaswellinfo.com
Email: ccalance@aol.com

ABSTRACT

I n the subsequent pages, I have presented information based on research from different sources and Scriptures from the Holy Bible which speaks eloquently for itself on the subject of God's Holy Sabbaths, feasts, laws, and commandments.

I tried not to interpret the Scriptures; rather, I allowed the Scripture to speak for itself. In addition, I have looked at the context, time and place as God's inspired Word was manifested through the writers of the various texts. I have used the spirit of discernment to obtain a clearer understanding of what was expressed.

CONTENTS

Introduction 9

1. The Beginning of the Sabbath 13

2. The Two Tablets 25

3. Sabbath—Old Testament (Tanakh) 29

4. Sabbath—New Testament (B 'rit Chadasha) 43

5. How the Sabbath Was Changed to Sunday
   and Truth From Church Leaders 47

6. Some Common Doctrines and Beliefs 65

7. Scriptural References About God's Laws
   and Commandments 89

8. Significant Feasts, Sabbaths, and Holy Days 97

9. Why the Sabbath Should Be Observed 111

10. Conclusion 131

Endnotes 143

Appendices 147

        A—The Names of God | 147

        B—Catholic Catechetical Formula
        of the Ten Commandments | 148

        C—Hebrew/Jewish Biblical or
        Sacred Calendar | 149

        D—Hebrew/Jewish Civil Calendar | 150

Scripture Index 151

About the Author 156

INTRODUCTION

For as long as I can remember, I have seen some people attending church on Saturday, the seventh day of the week, while the majority of people attend on Sunday, the first day of the week. Those who worship on Saturday regarded the seventh day as the Sabbath, and those who worshipped on Sunday considered the first day the Lord's day.

While growing up, I had a few relatives who worshipped on Saturday and others who worshipped on Sunday. The majority of my family, including me, worshipped on Sunday, and I always wondered which day it should be. I have been an ardent Sunday worshipper and a noted Messiah follower since 1987. I have listened to many preachers and their discussions regarding God's laws and commandments, but I have never heard any details mentioned about the seventh-day Sabbath.

In the spring of 2012, I felt the desire to rest and observe the seventh-day Sabbath, and as a result, I began a journey on my quest of finding the truth. In my discussions, God refers to "God the Father" and Yeshua (God-incarnate-man in flesh and Word) as "the Messiah," Who is known in this modern world as *Jesus,* which is from the Greek translation. God's holy name YHVH is the tetragrammaton of His sacred name that appears in the Scriptures and is pronounced "Yah-Heh-Vav-Heh" in Hebrew. Historically, only the high priests were allowed to use this name once a year on the Day of Atonement when he sought forgiveness for the sins of the people and himself. Several names, which are associated with God, give us meaning and reveal His nature and attributes or who God is to us. (See Appendix A.)The Bible declared in II Timothy 3:16 that *"All scripture is given by inspiration of God and is profitable for doctrine, for reproof, for correction, for instruction in righteousness."* Due to the fact that the Bible is the divinely inspired Word of God given to man, I decided to search the Scriptures to find out what the Bible says. As I turned the pages of the Scriptures book by book, I discovered that an abundance of passages refer to the Sabbath, the seventh day of the week, which forms a part of God's law and commandments. On the other hand, I discovered only eight references addressing the first day, Sunday.

As I continued to search the Scriptures I was impacted by the words found in Psalm 119:18 and 19, which say, *"Open thou my eyes, that I may behold wondrous things out of thy law. I am a stranger in the earth: hide not thy commandments from me."* As I continued to embark upon this amazing journey through the Bible, I was astounded as the Scriptures unraveled the tenets of God's instructions before my eyes in a very concise fashion. I have read all of the texts from Genesis to Revelation regarding God's holy Sabbaths, feasts, laws and commandments, and I am fully persuaded that they are an integral part of a person's worship, spirituality, and teaching to bring clarity to our belief, understanding, obedience and relationship with the true and living God.

Subsequent to the assassination and/or death of the disciples, apostles and other martyrs and by the beginning of the second century, it is noticeable that certain individuals, groups and leaders within the Roman Empire construed and presented Sunday as the Sabbath. By the end of the fourth century, the religious and political leaders had modified the commandments (See Appendix B.), which are God's prescription for living and had instead crafted holidays mingled with pagan rituals which seemingly overshadow God's Holy days. In addition to the seventh-day weekly Sabbath, seven additional Sabbath days are included in the annual feasts, which are purposefully ordained and significantly tied to the past, the present and the future.

In addition to my reading and comprehensive research, I wrote to several ministers of the Gospel who have established mega-churches in their communities from central Florida, Georgia, Texas and California, asking them if they observe the seventh-day Sabbath. These known and recognized Christian leaders and authors host national weekly television broadcasts, and some lead global ministries. The few who responded declared that Sunday is the Sabbath based on the day of Yeshua's (the Messiah's) resurrection. Reference was also made to some of Paul's teachings and doctrines to confirm their position.

The big question in my mind is: "Who do we obey?" Peter and the other disciples/apostles, while on trial before the High Priest and other members of the Jewish council, responded boldly and valiantly in chorus-like fashion: "... *We ought to obey God rather than men*" (Acts 5:29). Their response brings me to another valid point made by Peter according to Paul's teachings in II Peter 3:15, 16, which says:

———◆———

"Paul, according to the wisdom given to him as written to you, as also in all his epistles, speaking in them of these things, in which are some things hard to understand, which untaught and unstable people twist to their own destruction, as they do to the rest of the Scriptures."

The truth matters and will always prevail, so I believe it is right to seek the truth and align ourselves to God's instructions and expectations.

It is also necessary for individuals to comprehend and understand the truth and to be equipped to communicate this truth. Paul, in his letter of exhortation to young Timothy, said the following to him, *"Study to show thyself approved unto God a workman that needeth not be ashamed, rightly dividing the word of truth"* (2 Timothy 2:15). I have looked at the Scriptures and paid special attention to God's Word as it manifests through the various leaders, prophets, disciples and apostles. Strict attention was also given to the statements spoken by God and Yeshua, the Messiah.

In the light of my findings from the Bible and some historical data, I decided to write this information and provide a source for individuals to read and decide for themselves as my intention is not to condemn, criticize, or convert anyone. It is the sole responsibility of the Holy Spirit through Yeshua, the Messiah, to convict and convert. I am only a voice of conscience for His truth. Yeshua states that *"ye are the salt of the earth...ye are the light of the world"* (Matthew 5:13, 14).

CHAPTER ONE

THE BEGINNING
OF THE SABBATH

The book of beginnings—Genesis—chapters 1 and 2 speak of God's work of Creation. At the end of His six days' creative work, Genesis 1:31 records that He rested on the seventh day from all of His work. Genesis 2:3 declares that God blessed the seventh day and sanctified it because He had rested on this day from all of the work of Creation. This day of rest was not only blessed, but it was set apart as a holy day by and for God to be observed and honored by His children.

It is evident that from the foundation of the world that God instituted His laws and "gold standards" for righteous living. The first couple, Adam and Eve, violated God's command, resulting in sin entering the world. Seven generations later during the pre-flood era, Enoch, the father of Methuselah, was *transfigured* or "translated." He did not see death because he walked with God and faithfully pleased his Heavenly Father. Enoch conformed to the laws and commands of God while others lived in disobedience (Genesis 5:24, Hebrews 11:5, and Jude 1:14). Three generations later, the Bible declared that the great-grandson of Enoch, Noah, had found grace in the sight of God. He was a just man and perfect in all his generations, and he walked with God. As a result of the corruption, violence, wickedness and disobedience that existed at that time, Noah was given the audacious and daring venture by God to build an ark to save his family, animals and other creatures from the impending flood that would destroy man and all living things (Genesis 6, 7). God showed grace and mercy to Noah and, at the end of the flood, He established a covenant which is the sign of the rainbow, indicating that God will not destroy the world with another flood (Genesis 9:11-17).

In Luke 17:26, 27, Yeshua compared the time of Noah with the end times when He will return. Historical and geological data have confirmed that a global and catastrophic flood did indeed take place. Remnants of Noah's ark were said to be seen on Mt. Ararat in Turkey (www.Arkdiscovery.com). Genesis Chapter 10 outlined the generations of Noah and the regions of the Mediterranean and North Africa where they settled.

Abraham, the tenth generation from Noah, lived with his father and relatives in the fertile crescent of the Mesopotamia region of Sumer, later known as Babylon (present-day Iraq)—an area where the two great rivers, the Tigris and the Euphrates, were closest to each other. This region is considered the site of the earliest civilization, and the Sumerians worshiped many gods, including the sun. The Bible called the area "Ur of the Chaldees" (Genesis 11:31). Abraham was instructed by God to leave the area and to move to Canaan, present-day Israel and/or Palestine.

On Mount Moriah, Abraham displayed extraordinary faith when he willingly agreed to sacrifice his son Isaac. However, God provided a ram as a substitute that Abraham sacrificed on the altar. This sacrificial event represented the first act of the shedding of blood for the remission of sin and the offer of salvation. The ram's horn (the shofar), which is significant in Judaism, also symbolically foreshadows the trumpet that will herald in the return of the Messiah as King (Psalm 81:3-5, 1 Thessalonians 4:16). Abraham was chosen by God as the patriarch to lead his family in pursuit of a righteous living standard according to God's spoken laws and commandments. Genesis 26:5 states, *"Abraham obeyed my voice, kept my charge, my commandments, my statutes and my laws."* Consequently, from the testimony of this verse alone, I have no doubt that Abraham observed the Sabbath.

Abraham and his following descendants lived in Canaan (present-day Israel) for many years until Abraham's grandson

God provided a ram as a substitute for Abraham to sacrifice on the altar.

Jacob, the patriarch of the twelve tribes of Israel, and his entire clan of 70 joined his son Joseph in Egypt. There, Jacob's descendents remained for 430 years and increased to a population of approximately one million. The Hebrews/Israelites were enslaved for more than four hundred years.

On Mount Horeb, Moses was chosen by God to lead the Hebrews/Israelites out of Egypt to the Promised Land (or Canaan). The Passover instituted by God as a memorial culminated the last big event before their hurried departure. Their first stop after leaving Egypt was at Succoth where the children of Israel assembled before embarking on the wilderness journey.

Immediately after the miraculous event of the Red Sea crossing, Moses and the Hebrews/Israelites sang praises to God for delivering them from Pharaoh's pursuing army, and his sister Miriam and the women concluded with singing, dancing and playing the timbrels (Exodus 15:1-21). The children of Israel were without water after journeying in the wilderness for three days. At Marah they found water, but it was bitter. Moses then cried out to the Lord following the murmuring of the people, and the Lord showed him a tree. Moses cast the tree into the waters, and the waters were made sweet. God then spoke to them:

> "If you diligently heed the voice of the LORD your God and do what is right in His sight, give ear to His commandments and keep all His statutes, I will put none of the diseases on you which I have brought on the Egyptians, for I am the LORD who heals you" (Exodus 15:26).

During their pilgrimage from Egypt, the Hebrews/Israelites experienced the Sabbath before the Mt. Sinai encounter as out-

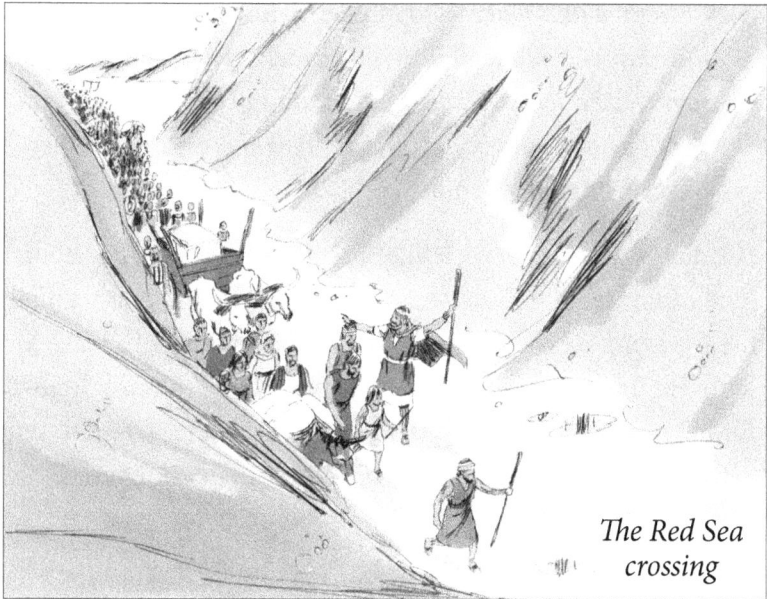

The Red Sea crossing

lined in Exodus Chapter 16. The children of Israel murmured against Moses and his brother Aaron in the wilderness of Sin regarding food. Exodus 16:4, 5 (KJV), state:

"Then said the LORD unto Moses, Behold I will rain bread from heaven for you; and the people shall go out and gather a certain rate every day and I will prove them if they will walk in my law, or no. And it shall come to pass that on the sixth day they shall prepare that which they shall bring in; and it shall be twice as much as they gather daily."

Moses and Aaron told the children of Israel that they would see the glory of the Lord because He had heard their murmurings. As they all gathered and looked toward the wilderness, they saw the glory of the Lord appear in the cloud.

"And the LORD spake unto Moses, saying, I have heard the murmurings of the children of Israel: speak unto them, saying, At even ye shall eat flesh, and in the morning ye shall be filled with bread; and ye shall know that I am the LORD your God" (Exodus 16:11, 12).

Exodus 16:17-30 chronicles the first observance of the Sabbath by the children of Israel. God provided quails and manna (daily bread) from Heaven. Moses instructed them not to leave any leftovers until morning. Some disobeyed and stored it, only to find that it had bred worms and smelled. On the sixth day, they gathered twice as much bread, and Moses said to them:

"…This is that which the LORD hath said, Tomorrow is the rest of the holy sabbath unto the LORD; bake that which ye will bake to day, and seethe that ye will seethe, and that which remaineth over lay up for you to be kept until the morning" (v. 23).

The next morning, which was the Sabbath, nothing stank or was infested with worms, and Moses said in verses 25 and 26:

"…Eat that to day; for to day is a sabbath unto the LORD: to day ye shall not find it in the field. Six days ye shall gather it; but on the seventh day, which is the Sabbath, in it there shall be none."

Some of the people disobeyed and went out on the seventh day to seek food but found nothing.

"And the LORD said unto Moses, How long refuse ye to keep my commandments and my laws? [29]See, for the LORD hath

given you the sabbath, therefore he giveth you on the sixth
day the bread of two days; abide ye every man in his place,
let no man go out of his place on the seventh day. [30]*So the*
people rested on the seventh day" (Exodus 16:28-30).

An omer or "six pints" of this manna bread was kept in a
pot as a testimony and was later placed in the Ark of the
Covenant (Exodus 16:33, 34). God instructed Moses to tell the
people to make preparation on the sixth day and to have enough
food put away for the Sabbath. Importantly, the Sabbath was observed before the Mount Sinai encounter where God spoke to
Moses and gave him the tablets with the law of covenants and
the Ten Commandments.

Exodus chapter 19 declared that Moses went up to Mount
Sinai where the Lord spoke to him. Verses 10 and 11 recorded
the following:

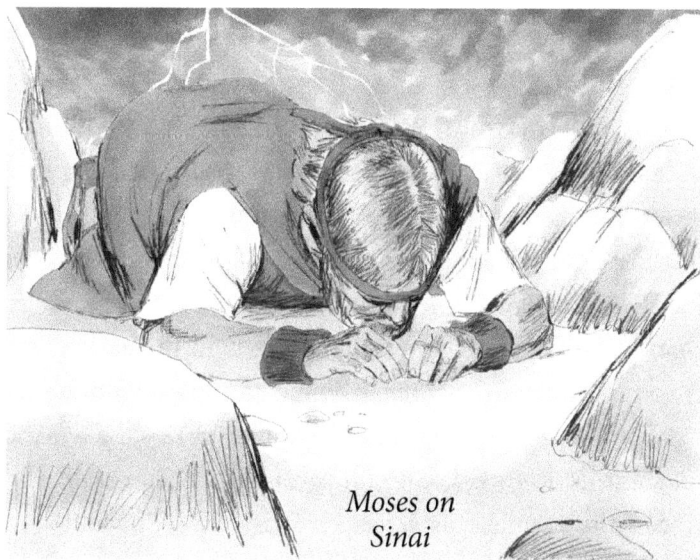

Moses on
Sinai

———◆———

"And the Lord said unto Moses, Go unto the people and sanctify them today and tomorrow and let them wash their clothes. And be ready against the third day; for the third day the Lord will come down in the sight of all the people upon Mt Sinai."

On the morning of the third day, the people trembled at the sight of lightning and a thick cloud upon the mountain and the sound of thunder and the exceedingly loud voice of a trumpet. Moses brought the people out of the camp, and they watched as the other side of Mt Sinai was covered with smoke and the ground was quaking as the Lord descended upon it.

"And when the voice of the trumpet sounded long, and waxed louder and louder, Moses spake, and God answered him by a voice. And the Lord came down upon mount Sinai, on the top of the mount: and the Lord called Moses up to the top of the mount; and Moses went up" (Exodus 19:19, 20).

God declared the words of the commandments as outlined in Exodus 20:1-17. As all of the people saw the thundering and the lightning and heard the noise of the trumpet, they were afraid of God's presence (Exodus 20:18). The rest of chapters 20 through 22 outlined the laws concerning God's altar, servants, violence, property, moral, and ceremonial matters. In the early chapters of Exodus 23, statements regarding justice for all and the law of the Sabbaths were portrayed, and Exodus 23:12 states, *"Six days thou shalt do thy work, and on seventh day thou shall rest...."* Three of the annual feasts, Pesach (Passover), Shavout (Pentecost), and Sukkot (Feast of Tabernacles) were also outlined. Hebrew/Israelite men had to appear in the temple at these feasts.

The Scriptures later declared that God told Moses that he, the seventy elders, Aaron and his sons should come and worship before Him, but only Moses should come near. They built an altar and twelve pillars at the foot of the mountain. Moses wrote all of the words spoken of the Lord. They offered burnt offerings and sacrifices of peace offerings to the Lord, and Moses sprinkled blood on the altar. Moses then took the book of the covenant and read it in the presence of the people. *"…And they said, All that the LORD hath said will we do, and be obedient"* (Exodus 24:7). Moses took the remainder of the blood and sprinkled it on the people, saying, *"…Behold the blood of the covenant, which the LORD hath made with you according all these words"* (Exodus 24:8).

Then the Lord said to Moses, *"…Come up to me into the mount, and be there; and I will give thee tablets of stone, and a law, and commandments which I have written; that thou mayest teach them"* (Exodus 24:12). Moses went up into the mountain, and a cloud covered the mountain.

"Now the glory of the LORD rested on Mount Sinai and the cloud covered it six days: and on the seventh day [or Sabbath], *He called unto Moses out of the midst of the cloud. The sight of the glory of the LORD was like a consuming fire on top of the mountain in the eyes of the children of Israel. So Moses went into the midst of the cloud, and went up into the mountain. And Moses was on the mountain forty days and forty nights* (Exodus 24:16-18).

Moses was called out on the Sabbath to begin his holy commune with God, and the description on that day revealed the glory of God.

God later spoke to Moses (Exodus 31:12-17) and outlined the Sabbath and instructed:

> "...*My Sabbaths he shall keep and it is a sign to be observed throughout your generations and I am the* LORD *who sanctifies it. Six days may work be done but the seventh day is a Sabbath of rest. The Sabbath should be observed holy and as a perpetual covenant and as a sign because in six days the* LORD *made the heaven and earth and on the seventh day He rested and was refreshed."*

Moses left Mount Sinai with the tablets of testimony—two tablets of stone containing the commandments and the covenants, which were written with the finger of God. While Moses was on the mountain, at the request of the people, Moses' brother Aaron constructed a golden calf, and they all began to worship. Exodus 32:19 states that,

> "...*So it was soon as he came near the camp that he saw the calf and the dancing. So Moses anger became hot, and he cast the tablets out of his hands and broke them at the foot of the mountain."*

Not only were the two stone tablets of the law of covenants and commandments broken by Moses, but the people also broke their covenant with God by their idolatrous worship.

In Exodus 34:1-4, God summoned Moses to cut two tablets of stone similar to the first ones and to return to Mount Sinai and present himself before God. Moses did so, and the Scriptures stated,

> "And the LORD passed by before him, and proclaimed, The LORD, The LORD God, merciful and gracious, longsuffering, and abundant in goodness and truth. Keeping mercy for thousands, forgiving iniquity and transgression and sin, and that will by no means clear the guilty; visiting the iniquity of the fathers upon the children, and upon the children's children, and unto the third and to the fourth generation" (Exodus 34:6, 7; KJV).

Moses bowed and worshipped and remained with God for another 40 days and 40 nights, and during this time, the covenants and commandments were renewed, which illustrates God's gift of forgiveness and offer of redemption.

Exodus 34:29 and 30 share that when Moses returned from the mount with the second set of tablets that the skin of his face

shone. Aaron and all of the people were afraid to come near him. However, Moses called out to them, and when they came closer, Moses talked with them about the things God had commanded and had written on the two stone tablets.

THE TWO TABLETS

The Ten Commandments
(Exodus 20 and Deuteronomy 5)

1. *"Thou shall have no other gods before me"* (Exodus 20:3).
2. *"Thou shall not make unto thee any graven image, or any likeness of anything that is in the heaven above or that is in the earth beneath or that is in the water under the earth. Thou shall not bow down thyself to them, nor serve them: for I am the* LORD *thy God am a jealous God visiting the iniquity of the fathers upon the children unto the third and fourth generation of them that hate me. And showing mercy unto thousands of them that love me, and keep my commandments."* (Exodus 20:4-6)
3. *"Thou shall not take the name of the* LORD *thy God in vain; for the* LORD *will not hold him guiltless that taketh his name in vain"* (Exodus 20:7).
4. *"Remember the Sabbath day to keep holy. ⁹Six days shalt thou labor and do all thy work; ¹⁰but the seventh day is the Sabbath of the* LORD *God: in it thou shalt not do any work, thou, nor thy son, nor thy daughter, nor thy maidservant, nor thy cattle, nor thy stranger that is within thy gates: ¹¹For in six days the* LORD *made the heaven and earth, the sea, and all that in them is, and rested on the*

———◆———

seventh day: wherefore the LORD blessed the Sabbath day and hallowed it" (Exodus 20:8-11).

5. "Honor thy father and thy mother that thy days may be long upon the land which the LORD thy God giveth thee" (Exodus 20:12).

6. "Thou shall not kill" (Exodus 20:13).

7. "Thou shall not commit adultery" (Exodus 20:14).

8. "Thou shall not steal" (Exodus 20:15).

9. "Thou shall not bear false witness against thy neighbor" (Exodus 20:16).

10. "Thou shall not covet thy neighbor's house; thou shall not covet thy neighbor's wife, nor his manservant, nor his ox, nor his ass, nor anything that is thy neighbor's" (Exodus 20:17).

The Laws of Covenants
(Exodus 24:12; 34:10-28).

1. God will drive out the people from the Promised Land and enlarge their borders.

2. Moses will destroy the altars, sacred pillars, and wooden images of the people in the land.

3. They shall worship no other God because the Lord Jehovah is a jealous God.

4. They shall make no molded gods.

5. The Sabbath is to be observed—six days of work and rest on the seventh.

6. The people are to observe the three yearly feasts: the

Passover/the Feast of Unleavened Bread, the Feast of First Fruits or Harvest/Feast of Weeks/Pentecost, and the Feast of Ingathering or Tabernacle—at the year's end.

7. All of the men are to appear before the Lord three times a year.

8. Blood sacrifices should not be offered with leaven.

9. Passover sacrifices should not be left over until the morning.

10. The first fruits of the land are to be brought to the house of the Lord, and do not seethe a kid in his mother's milk.

Exodus 35:2 and 3 indicated that Moses gathered together all of the people and reaffirmed to them the words as commanded by the Lord; in particular, that work should be done in six days, but the seventh day shall be a Holy Day—a Sabbath of rest to the Lord. No fires should be kindled in the people's dwellings on the Sabbath.

In addition to the stone tablets containing the laws of covenants and commandments, the first 23 chapters of the book of Leviticus outline the ceremonial laws concerning sacrifices, offerings, diet, priestly duties and responsibilities. These chapters also make reference to personal and national cleanliness, holiness and the laws pertaining to the three annual feasts. Additionally, constant reminders of the Sabbath can be found in the following Scriptures.

- In Leviticus 22:31 this instruction is given: *"Therefore shall ye keep my commandments, and do them; I am the LORD."*

- Leviticus 23:3 states: *"Six days shall work be done: but the seventh day is a Sabbath of solemn rest or holy convocation. You shall do no work in it. It is the Sabbath of the LORD in all your dwellings."*

The remainder of this chapter speaks about the annual feasts including the special holy Sabbaths, and verse 32 is a reminder that the Sabbath is from sunset to sunset.

- Leviticus 19:30 and 26:2 also states that, *"Ye shall keep my Sabbaths, and reverence my sanctuary: I am the LORD."* The final four chapters of Leviticus focus on God's promises for keeping the law as well as His warnings for violating them.

CHAPTER THREE

SABBATH—OLD TESTAMENT [TANAKH]

After Moses and the Hebrews/Israelites came out of the Sinai wilderness, they settled on the plains of Moab. While living among the Moabites, some who were in disobedience to God began to participate in idol worship. Consequently, Moses reviewed the Ten Commandments, and in Deuteronomy 5: 12-15, the Sabbath is fully explained:

> *"Keep the Sabbath day to sanctify it, as the LORD thy God has commanded thee. Six days thou shall labor and do all thy work. But the seventh day is the Sabbath of the LORD thy God, in it thou shall not do any work. It's a day of complete rest."*

Moses in reaffirming the relevance and importance of God to the Hebrews/Israelites said,

> *"Hear, O Israel; The LORD our God is one LORD; ⁵And thou shall love the LORD thy God with all thine heart, and with all thy soul, and with all thy might. ⁶And these words which I command thee this day shall be in thine heart: ⁷And thou shall teach them diligently unto thy children, and shalt talk of them when thou sittest in thine house,*

and when thou walkest by the way, and when thou liest down, and when thou riseth up. ⁸And thou shalt bind them for a sign upon thine hand, and they shall be as frontlets between thine eyes. ⁹And thou shall write them upon the posts of thy house, and on thy gates" (Deuteronomy 6:4-9).

The preceding verses, which are called the SHEMA, are the central prayer in Jewish worship and usually the first prayer a Jewish child is taught. It is a declaration of faith and illustrates a commitment to one God. Most Messianic and some Gentile believers also say this prayer. Yeshua, in answering the scribes, referenced this Scripture and alluded to the fact that this is the first and greatest commandment as stated in Mark 12:29-31, which says,

"...The first of all the commandments is, Hear, O Israel; The Lord our God is one Lord: ³⁰And thou shalt love the Lord thy God with all thy heart, and with all thy soul, and with all thy mind, and with all thy strength: this is the first commandment. ³¹And the second is like, namely this, Thou shalt love thy neighbour as thyself...." (See also Matthew 22:36-40 and Luke 10:25-27.)

After the death of Moses, Joshua, the new leader, in another miraculous event led the people across the Jordon River to the Promised Land and allocated the land according to the twelve tribes of Israel. (See adjacent map.)

THE TWELVE TRIBES
OF ISRAEL
Around 1200-1050 B.C.

For more than 400 years, the Hebrews/Israelites enjoyed a level of prosperity despite neighboring feuds, leadership struggles, moral and spiritual decline. At the end of King David's reign, his son Solomon succeeded him to the throne, and in seven years he built the magnificent temple at Mt. Moriah—the location where God provided Abraham with the sacrificial ram in lieu of Isaac. At the completion of the Temple, Solomon held a seven-day Feast of Dedication, followed by the seven-day Feast of Tabernacles, culminating with a solemn assembly on the eighth day. Solomon offered a significant prayer of dedication. The Scriptures declared that God appeared to Solomon and told the king that He heard his prayers, and additionally said these words:

"If My people who are called by My name will humble themselves, and pray and seek My face and turn from their wicked ways, then I will hear from heaven and I will forgive their sin and heal their land." Now My eyes will be open and My ears attentive to the prayer made in this place" (2 Chronicles 7:14, 15).

Verses 19 and 20 stated the following warnings:

"But if you turn away and forsake my statutes and My commandments which I have set before you, and go and serve other gods and worship them, 'then I will uproot them from My land which I have given them; and this house which I have sanctified for My name I will cast out of My sight and I will make it a proverb and a byword among all peoples' " (See also 1 Kings 9:6-9.).

Shortly after the end of King Solomon's reign, the kingdom of Israel was divided into two separate kingdoms with Judah and its capital city Jerusalem in the south, consisting of the tribes of Judah and Benjamin as well as the priests and the Levites. The remaining ten tribes occupied the northern region representing the kingdom of Israel and its capital Samaria. Many prophets including Amos, Isaiah and Ezekiel warned both kingdoms of their disobedience to God. During the time of the prophet Hosea, the northern kingdom (Israel) enjoyed some prosperity, but there was much moral corruption and spiritual adultery. In Hosea 2:11, the prophet warned them about many of their sinful practices including the profaning of the Sabbath. Hosea even went on to make the following pronouncement:

"My people are destroyed for lack of knowledge, because you have rejected knowledge. I will also reject you from being priest for me; because you have forgotten the law of your God. I will also forget your children" (Hosea 4:6).

The ten tribes of the kingdom of Israel were ultimately taken into Assyrian captivity between 744 B.C. and about 726 B.C., launching the massive dispersion of the Hebrews/Israelites to various parts of the world as well as the occupation of their land in Samaria and other townships by the Babylonians and people from other regions. (See 2 Kings 17.) The prophet Jeremiah also warned the southern kingdom of Judah that because the people had broken God's covenant, they would face calamity (Jeremiah 11:10, 11). Habakkuk, a minor prophet, was also overwhelmed with the situation in Judea and, in crying out to God, he questioned as to how long such indignation would exist. In

———◆———

Habakkuk 1:5 and 6, God responded to his brokenhearted prophet:

> *"Look among the nations and watch. Be utterly astounded! For I will work a work in your days which you will not believe, though it were told you. For indeed I am raising the Chaldeans, a bitter, and hasty nations which marches through the breadth of the earth, to possess dwelling places that are not theirs."*

Many years later in approximately 586 B.C., the Chaldeans (Babylonians) captured Judah in the south, destroyed the Temple which had been built by King Solomon, and took the young and most promising of the people as captives to Babylon. (See 2 Kings 24.)

The words written in 1 Chronicles 9:1 confirmed that the Babylonian captivity was due to their unfaithfulness and was also a revelation of the warnings that God had pronounced to King Solomon several hundred years earlier after Solomon's prayer and dedication of the Temple. In 2 Chronicles 36:17-21, it is written,

> "*Therefore He brought against them the King of the Chaldeans... And those who escaped from the sword he carried away to fulfill the word of the LORD by the mouth of Jeremiah until the land had enjoyed her Sabbaths. As long as she lay desolate she kept the Sabbath, to fulfill seventy years.*"

The preceding Scriptures make reference to the Sabbath of the seventh year when the land should have been rested from agricultural activities (See Leviticus 25:1-8.). After the Persians conquered Babylon, King Cyrus issued an edict allowing the people from Judah (now called Jews) to return home, but some went to other parts of the Persian Empire. About 50,000 returned to Jerusalem and other towns of Judah after being in exile for 70 years, fulfilling God's promise to return His people after 70 years as prophesied by Jeremiah. The prophet Isaiah also made a similar proclamation about 150 years earlier. (See Isaiah 44:28; 45:1, 7.)

Zerubbabel, who was appointed governor of Judah by Cyrus, led the first wave of exiles to Judah and with their efforts as well as the support of the king of Persia, the Jerusalem temple was rebuilt after much resistance. Ezra, a scribe and priest, led the second group of exiles from captivity comprised of the priests and Levites. Subsequently, the Temple was dedicated, and the people began to worship God and celebrate the Passover and other Feasts. Ezra read the law to the whole assembly. *"...For all the people wept, when they heard the words of the law"* (Nehemiah 8:9; KJV). Ezra was very instrumental in bringing about spiritual reforms and restoring the spiritual condition of the people.

Nehemiah, who later became the governor of Judah, was granted leave by King Artaxerxes of Persia to return to Jerusalem. He led the third and last exodus to Jerusalem. He was deeply concerned when he heard about the depressing condition of the city of Jerusalem, and he took action and had the walls of Jerusalem rebuilt in 52 days in spite of internal and external opposition. Nehemiah also embarked upon a spiritual restoration among the people. Nehemiah Chapter 9 states that the people confessed their sins and worshipped Yahweh their God. The Levites (priests), during their adoration to God, spoke about the commandments and the Sabbath as stated in verses 13 and 14:

> *"You came down on Mount Sinai; you spoke to them from heaven. You gave them regulations and laws that are just and right, and decrees and command that are good. [14] You made known to them your holy Sabbath and gave them commands, decrees, and laws through your servant Moses your servant."* (Nehemiah 9:13, 14; NIV)

Chapter 10 addresses how Nehemiah and the people signed a covenant to uphold the laws and to observe the Sabbath. Nehemiah returned to the king of Persia for a period of time, but he returned to Jerusalem as soon as he received leave from the king. Upon his return to Jerusalem, he was very displeased at what he found and had to re-establish some reforms because the people did not live up to certain obligations and expectations. One major violation was their dishonoring the Sabbath by allowing merchants and sellers to do business on the Sabbath (Nehemiah 13:17, 18).

In Isaiah 1:10-20, reference is made about the people of Sodom and Gomorrah (cities destroyed by God) and how the Lord was displeased with their sacrifices, feasts and Sabbaths because of the way they were living. It is important to observe the Sabbaths of God, but every person's lifestyle should be a model of His truth and holiness. The following are references regarding the proper observance and blessings of the Sabbath as recorded in book of Isaiah by the prophet Isaiah.

Thus says the LORD: "Keep justice, and do righteousness, For My salvation is about to come, And My righteousness to be revealed. ²Blessed is the man who does this, and the son of man who lays hold on it; who keeps from defiling the Sabbath, and keeps his hand from doing any evil"... ⁴For thus says the LORD: to the eunuchs who keep My Sabbaths, and choose what pleases Me, and hold fast My covenant, ⁵Even to them I will give in My house and within My walls a place and a name better than that of sons and daughters; I will give them an everlasting name that shall not be cut off. ⁶"Also the sons of the foreigner who join themselves to the LORD, to serve Him, and to love the name of the LORD, to be his servants—everyone who keeps from defiling the Sabbath, and holds fast My covenant—⁷Even them I will bring to My holy mountain, and make them joyful in My house of prayer. Their burnt offerings and their sacrifices will be accepted on My altar; for My house shall be called the house of prayer for all nations." ⁸The LORD God, who gathers the outcasts of Israel, says, "Yet I will gather to him, others beside those who are gathered to him" (Isaiah 56:1-8; NKJV).

These words proclaimed by Isaiah instruct that the Sabbath is for everyone—not for the Jews or Hebrews/Israelites alone or the descendants of Jacob—but for all nations. Blessed is the man who observes the Sabbath and does not profane or defile it. The Sabbath is defiled when it is treated as an ordinary day. God set aside the Sabbath as a holy day; therefore, it is profaned when believers labor and do unnecessary tasks or unworthy deeds instead of spending time in God's presence with worship and praise.

Any foreigner who has joined himself to Jehovah is not to think of himself separate from God's people. He is adopted into the House of Israel; he is made part of it; he is entered into God's covenants; he is much a part of God's people as the native born Israelite....All people—no matter what their nationality—are invited to join themselves to Jehovah, to minister to Him, to love His name and to be His servants. His promise to those who will keep from profaning the Sabbath and hold fast to His covenant, is to bring them to His holy mountain (the kingdom of God) and make them joyful in His house of prayer.[1]

Isaiah 58:13 and 14 (NKJV) affirms,

"If you turn away your foot from the Sabbath, from doing your pleasure on My holy day, and call the Sabbath a delight, the holy day of the LORD honorable, and shall honor Him, not doing your own ways, nor finding your own pleasure, nor speaking your own words, ¹⁴Then you shall delight yourself in the LORD, and I will cause you to ride on the high hills of the earth, And feed you with the heritage of Jacob your father. The mouth of the LORD has spoken."

The preceding verses teach that the Sabbath must be recognized as a joy—not a burden. It is a shadow of the true delight that believers will have with Him in the future. The Sabbath is not a day for believers to seek their own pleasure by engaging in sporting activities, shopping and events that have the flavor of a holiday and ignore the purpose and true meaning of the Sabbath. The Sabbath is a holy day and was set apart for God and by God as an honorable day in which He must be honored.

Most people do not honor the Sabbath. Friday night is known for its great party and entertainment atmosphere, while Saturday is predominantly the busiest shopping day, involvement in all kinds of activities and taking care of household tasks. God's Sabbath is also to be honored by not speaking our own words but to seek that which is God. This day of rest should be one of prayer, thanksgiving, Bible study, and fellowship.

Isaiah 66:23 states, *" 'And it shall come to pass that from one new moon to another, and from one Sabbath to another, all flesh* shall come to worship before me,' says the LORD." This text reveals the continuity of the Sabbath, which is an everlasting covenant to be observed in honor, praise and worship to God. The Sabbath will be observed in the future kingdom of God. In Jeremiah 17:19-27, the prophet exhorted the people that the Sabbath day must be hallowed and doing business is forbidden. Jeremiah 31:31-33 expresses God's desire to enter into a new covenant by putting his law in their minds and writing it on their hearts. This prophecy was reiterated and revealed in the New Testament (B'rit Chadasha) times. (See Hebrews 8:7-12; 10:15-17.)

Ezekiel 20:12 states, *"Moreover also I gave them Sabbaths to be a sign between me and them that they might know that I am the LORD that sanctify them."* Ezekiel, in his prophetic writings, spoke several times about the disobedience of the children of Israel in violating God's Law and how they had polluted and profaned the Sabbath. However, restoration was promised despite God's harsh dealings toward them. Throughout the remaining books of the Old Testament (Tanakh), many emphatic statements express the laws, commandments, statutes and judgment of God, which will be highlighted later.

The following Psalm was designated as a song of praise to the Lord for His love and faithfulness to be rendered on the Sabbath day.

"It is good to give thanks to the Lord,
And to sing praises to your name, O Most High,
²To declare your loving kindness in the morning,
And your faithfulness every night,
³On an instrument of ten strings, on the lute,
And on the harp, with harmonious sound.

———◆———

⁴For you, LORD has made me glad through work.
I will triumph in the works of your hands.
⁵O LORD how great are your works,
Your thoughts are very deep.
⁶A senseless man does not know,
Nor does a fool understand this.
⁷When the wicked spring up like grass,
And when all the workers of iniquity flourish,
⁸It is that they may be destroyed forever.
But you, LORD or on high forevermore.
⁹For behold, Your enemies, O LORD,
For behold, Your enemies shall perish:
¹⁰All the workers of iniquity shall be scattered.
But my horn You have exalted like a wild ox;
¹¹I have been anointed with fresh oil.
My eye also has seen my desire on my enemies;
¹²My ears hear my desire on the wicked
Who rise up against me?
¹³The righteous shall flourish like a palm tree,
He shall grow like a cedar in Lebanon,
¹⁴Those who are planted in the house of the Lord
Shall flourish in the courts of our God.
¹⁵They shall still bear fruit in old age;
They shall be fresh and flourishing,
¹⁶To declare that the LORD is upright;
He is my rock, and there is no unrighteousness in Him."

(Psalm 92)

In the final book of the Old Testament (Tanakh), Malachi one of the minor prophets said:

"Remember the Law of Moses My servant, which I commanded him in Horeb for all Israel, with the statutes and judgments. Behold I will send you Elijah the prophet, before the coming of the great and dreadful day of the Lord" (Malachi 4:4, 5).

This statement made by Malachi makes it very clear that the commandments of God are not to be taken lightly and will be in reckoning in the future shortly before the return of Yeshua-Messiah, the King of the universe, to establish His kingdom.

CHAPTER FOUR

SABBATH—NEW TESTAMENT [B'RIT CHADASHA]

everal references are made about the Sabbath in the New Testament (B'rit Chadasha). In both Mark 2:27, 28 and Luke 6:5, a statement is given that some believers like to quote when the issue of the Sabbath observance is raised: *"the Sabbath is made for man and not man for the Sabbath."* In responding to the Pharisees who challenged Him for plucking ears of corn on the Sabbath, Yeshua, the Messiah, implores them in the presence of His disciples that *"the Sabbath was made for man and not man for the Sabbath and that He was LORD over the Sabbath."* Yeshua was making it clear to the Pharisees that the Sabbath was ordained for man to observe as God had intended and not for man to attach their own sabbatical laws.

Indeed, several manmade laws were attached. For example, one of these laws stated that a person could not walk any farther than two-fifths of a mile on the Sabbath (a Sabbath day's journey, Acts 1:12)—the distance from Mount Olivet to the Temple. Yeshua, the Messiah was also emphasizing that God created and blessed the Sabbath; therefore, He has the authority to govern the Sabbath. Yeshua indicated also by His actions that it was acceptable to do acts of mercy or certain necessities on the Sabbath

(Matthew 12:12; Luke 13:15, 16). Yeshua kept the Sabbath, and in Mark 6:2 Yeshua is mentioned as teaching in the synagogue on the Sabbath day.

All four Gospels outlined several instances about the Sabbath, which will be highlighted later. The disciples and the apostles all worshipped and observed the seventh-day Sabbath, and the day was not merely for the Jews but for all believers.

> *"So when the Jews went out of the synagogue, the Gentiles begged that these words might be preached to them the next Sabbath....On the next Sabbath almost the whole city came out to hear the word of God"* (Acts 13:42-44).

The seventh-day Sabbath is mentioned about 62 times in the New Testament (B'rit Chadasha) and twice as many times in the Old Testament (Tanakh) while the first day of the week is mentioned only eight times in the New Testament (B'rit Chadasha) as follows:

- Matthew 28:1
- Mark 16:9
- John 20:1
- Acts 20:7, 8
- Mark 16:1, 2
- Luke 24:1
- John 20:19
- 1 Corinthians 16:1-4

The first five texts clearly state that the women came to the sepulcher early in the morning after the Sabbath and discovered that Yeshua was not there because He resurrected. John 20:19 states that while the disciples were assembled behind closed doors because they feared the Jews, Yeshua appeared to them later on that resurrection day and said, *"Peace be still."* It is not hard to understand why they appeared scared and were locked behind closed doors. Having seen their Master-Teacher crucified, they were uncertain of their own fate. There is no suggestion from the text of a church service and the other Scriptures that relate to this meeting with the disciples only suggest they were eating. The Bible declared that over 500 people saw Yeshua, the Messiah, during the post-resurrection period (1 Corinthians 15:5-8) including two Marys, the two with whom He spoke on the road to Emmaus, the disciples, and the apostles, James and Paul. No evidence can be found in the Scriptures that Yeshua instructed them that the seventh-day Sabbath was to be changed from this day forward (as of the day of His resurrection).

Acts 20:7 and 8 state that the disciples came to break bread on the first day of week. Paul was having discussion with them at the conclusion of his seven-day mission trip at Troas. He was scheduled to depart the next morning. This meeting was at the end of the Sabbath after sunset which was now the first day (Saturday night). The Bible declares in Genesis 1:31 and Leviticus 23:32 that the evening which begins the dark part of a day (night) comes first, which is why a day is from one sunset to the next sunset. Many lights were in the upper room, and the meeting continued until midnight. In Acts 20:9 and 10, a young man named Eutychus, who was sitting in a window, had fallen asleep and fell from the third loft and appeared dead. Paul fell on him, embraced him and declared that he was not dead. Verse 11 records that they went back to the room, broke more bread and talked a long while till the break of day (Sunday morning) when they all departed. It is customary for the fellowship of eating to take place at the end of the Sabbath. Today, the Messianic and most other congregations who worship on the Sabbath day engage in a fellowship of sharing and eating at the end of their worship service.

> 1 Corinthian 16:1-4, *"Now concerning the collection for the saints, as I have given order to the churches in Galatia, even so do ye. ²Upon the first day of the week let every one of you lay by him in store, as God has prospered him, that there be no gatherings when I come. ³And when I come, whosoever he shall approve by your letters, them will I send to bring your liberality unto Jerusalem. ⁴And if it be meet that I go also, they shall go with me."*

Verse 3 indicated that their contributions were to be collected for the Jerusalem saints who were experiencing hardship or famine. Their contribution or free gifts could be taken by whomever they would approve, but Paul also expressed his willingness to go with the emissaries if necessary. The text made no mention of a "church service" the word being preached or the Torah's being read. Paul was visiting the other churches in the region, and he was asking the Corinthians' church to be generous also. (See also Acts 11:27-30 and Romans 15:25-28.) Obviously the first day of the week would be a good time to take a collection for these needs, as this collecting would not be done on the seventh day (Saturday)—the Sabbath—but most likely, they would be reminded of the needs of the Jerusalem church.

HOW THE SABBATH WAS CHANGED TO SUNDAY
and Truth From Religious Leaders

J ohn 1:1 says, *"In the beginning was the Word, and the Word was with God, and the Word was God.... 3All things were made by him; and without him was not any thing made that was made"* (vv. 1, 3).

God ended His work of Creation and rested on the seventh day from all of His labor. Then God blessed the seventh day and sanctified it (Genesis 2:2, 3). God set apart this seventh day, which is known to be Saturday, as His Holy Sabbath and for humankind to rest from their labors, honor and obey Him. For more than three thousand years, the seventh day was observed as the Sabbath.

Following the death, resurrection and ascension of Yeshua, the Messiah, in the spring of A.D. 30, on the day of Shavout/Pentecost, the Holy Spirit converted three thousand souls, launching the Messianic era (believers in Messiah). The disciples and the apostles, with Peter and Paul as the major evangelists, presented the message of the Yeshua-Messiah in a fashion that integrated both Jewish and Gentile believers. Therefore, during the early years, the church was Messianic in nature, and they consistently followed the teachings and ways of Yeshua-Messiah.

The resistance by the political and pagan culture gave rise to the persecution of many followers of Yeshua-Messiah, including the disciples and the apostles. Subsequently, many including Peter and Paul were tortured and killed by the end of the first century. The following information according to church history revealed the disciples and apostles who were among the early martyrs.

- James, the brother of John, was killed in Jerusalem, A.D. 44.
- Philip was crucified in Phrygia, A.D. 54.
- Matthew was beheaded in Ethiopia, A.D. 60.
- Barnabas was burned to death in Cyprus, A.D. 64.
- Mark was dragged to death in Alexandria, A.D. 64.
- James (the Just, the brother of Yeshua) was clubbed to death in Jerusalem, A.D. 66.
- Paul was beheaded in Rome, A.D. 66.
- Peter was crucified in Rome, A.D. 69.
- Andrew was crucified in Achaia, A.D. 70.
- Thomas was speared to death in Calamina, A.D. 70.
- Luke was hanged in Athens, A.D. 95.[1]

The willingness of the disciples and the apostles to face death rather than denying Yeshua-Messiah is evidence of their strong belief and eyewitness account to seeing the resurrected Messiah. The persecution and execution also fulfilled the words of the Yeshua-Messiah.

Research reveals that toward the middle of the second century, Sunday worship began in Rome and later spread to other parts of the Roman Empire. Roman writers began to attack the observance of Sabbath, God's perpetual covenant with His people. Saint Justin Martyr (100-165 A.D.), a philosopher and a defender of the Christian faith, condemned the Sabbath observance and provided the earliest account of the "Lord's Day" Sunday worship.[2]

Constantine the Great

In 313 A.D. Constantine, the emperor of Rome, issued the Edict of Milan, making Christianity a legal religion. Christians could now worship freely without the fear of persecution. Pope Sylvester (314–335 A.D.) declared Sunday as the "Lord's Day," and then the church leaders later regarded the seventh-day Sabbath as a Jewish custom. In 321 A.D. Constantine then passed a Sunday law, making the day a public holiday. That law reads as follows:

On the venerable day of the sun let the magistrates and people residing in the cities rest and let all the workshops be closed. In the country however persons engaged in agriculture may freely and lawfully continue their pursuits because it often happens that another day is not suitable for grain sowing or vine planting; lest by neglecting the proper moment for such operations the bounty of heaven be lost.[3]

After the Emperor Constantine made Christianity the official religion in the Roman Empire, he allowed the merger of pagan practices with Christian beliefs in order to maintain power and control.

In his book, *The Two Babylons*, which was written one hundred years ago, Alexander Heslop explained this religious syncretism, by stating, "To conciliate pagans to nominal Christianity, pursuing its usual policy took measures to get Christians and pagan festivals amalgamated and by a complicated but skillful adjustment of the calendar. It was found no difficult matter."

As Christianity began to coexist in a dominant pagan culture, it branded and blended certain ideas and made changes; the days of the week were not exempt. The names for the days of the week were then derived from the heavenly bodies:

- Sunday (sun)
- Monday (moon)
- Tuesday (Mars)
- Wednesday (Mercury)
- Thursday (Jupiter)
- Friday (Venus)
- Saturday (Saturn)

Prior to this renaming of the days of the week, throughout the known world, the seven days were simply called the first day, the second day, the third day, the fourth day, the fifth day, the sixth day, and the seventh day—regardless of the language spoken.

In A.D. 364 at the council of Laodicea, the Catholic church agreed that the observance of the seventh day Sabbath was forbidden, and Christians were to worship on Sunday. A group of thirty church leaders from regions of the Roman Empire who were in attendance formulated the doctrine of the church comprised of 60 Canons (Laws), which portray the rules and regulations to govern the church. The reading of Canon xxix (29) is as follows:

> *Christians must not* Judaize by resting on the Sabbath, but must work on that day, rather Honoring the Lord's Day; and if they can, resting then as Christians. But if any shall be found to be Judaizers, let them be anathema from Christ.[4]

This statement is not only a violation of the fourth commandment, but it appears that the council of leaders believed they had the power to make it a curse or excommunicate one from Yeshua, the Messiah, for being obedient to the commands of God and failing to adhere to the rules of the church prescribed by man.

By the fifth century A.D., a time when both Saturday and Sunday worship was observed and followed, the intent of Rome was to terminate Sabbath observance. Pope Gregory (A.D. 590-604) demanded all secular activities to be ceased on Sunday so that people could devote time to prayer, and by the twelfth century, Sunday became the substitute for the seventh-day (Saturday) Sabbath. For more than one thousand years, Roman Catholicism remained the dominant religion throughout the Christian world, and its impact was both significant and devastating.

Not until the sixteenth century after Martin Luther, on the eve of All Saints' Day on October 31, 1517, nailed his 95 theses, The Power and Efficacy of Indulgences, on the door of Castle Church of Wittenberg, Germany, because of the conflict over indulgences and penitence that the Reformation truly began. New converts of the Catholic church had to purchase the book of indulgence as part of the repentance process and acceptance into the church.

The Protestant Reformation, the movement of separation from the Catholic church, which gave rise to numerous Christian denominations was largely due to doctrine and governance. Today, several centuries later, the world has a menu of Christian denominations in every nook and cranny of the Christian world. However, on the issue of the seventh-day Sabbath, they indeed accepted tradition over truth. Martin Luther and other reformers were highly ridiculed by the Catholic church for their views on some issues; however, they all upheld Sunday the first day of the week as the significant day of worship instead of Saturday, the seventh day of the week, as the Sabbath. Dr. Samuele Bacchiocchi, a former professor at Andrews University and author of several books, wrote in an article, "How Did Church on Sunday Begin?" and concluded the following:

The change from Saturday to Sunday was not simply one of names and numbers, but of authority, meaning and experience. It was a change from a holy day divinely established to enable us to experience more freely and more fully, the awareness of divine presence and peace in our lives, into a holiday that has become an occasion to seek for personal pleasure and profit. This historical change has greatly affected the quality of Christian life of countless Christians deprived throughout the centuries of the physical, moral, spiritual renewal the Sabbath provides. Needed today is the recovery of the Sabbath when our souls, fragmented, penetrated and desiccated by a cacophonous, tension-filled culture, cry out for the release and realignment that awaits us on the Sabbath Day.[5]

What the Church/Religious Leaders Revealed

ROMAN CATHOLICS

Cardinal James Gibbons, the archbishop of Baltimore (1876-1921), wrote the following:

> *You may read* the Bible from Genesis to Revelation, and you will not find a single line authorizing the sanctification of Sunday. The Scriptures enforce the religious observance of Saturday, a day which we never sanctified.[6]

He also declared: "…the Catholic Church…By the virtue of her divine mission, changed the day from Saturday to Sunday."[7]

> *Had she not* such power, she could not have done that in which all modern religionists agree with her, she could not have substituted the observance of Sunday, the

first day of the week, for the observance of Saturday the seventh day, a change for which there is no scriptural authority.[8]

The papacy in Rome has claimed the authority to make changes to the God's law.

The Pope is of so great authority and power that he can modify, explain or interpret even divine laws…The Pope can modify divine law, since his power is not of man, but of God, and he acts as vice-regent of God upon earth.[9]

The Protestant world has been from its infancy in the sixteen century in thorough accord with the Catholic church in keeping "holy" not Saturday but Sunday.[10]

If Protestants would follow the Bible, they should worship God on the Sabbath day that is Saturday. In keeping Sunday they are following a law of the Catholic Church.[11]

It [the Roman Catholic Church] reversed the fourth commandment by doing away with the Sabbath of God's word and instituting Sunday as a holiday.[12]

"*To tell you* the Truth,…for example, nowhere in the Bible do we find that Christ or the Apostles ordered that the Sabbath be changed from Saturday to Sunday. We have the commandments of God given to Moses to keep holy the Sabbath day that is the 7th day of the week, Saturday. Today most Christians keep Sunday because it has been revealed to us by the (Roman Catholic) church outside of the Bible."[13]

The following questions and answers were depicted in an autograph letter by Cardinal Gibbons in 1906.

1. "Is Saturday the 7th day according to the Bible and the 10 Commandments?"
   I answer, "Yes."
2. "Is Sunday the first day of the week and did the church changed the 7th day Sabbath for Sunday the 1st day?"
   I answer, "Yes."
3. "Did Christ change the day?"
   I answer, "No."[14]

Question: "Which is the Sabbath day?"
Answer: "Saturday is the Sabbath day."
Question: "Why do we observe Sunday instead of Saturday?"
Answer: "We observe Sunday instead of Saturday because the Catholic Church transferred the solemnity from Saturday to Sunday."[15]

T. Enright, C.S.S.R., in a February 1884 lecture at Hartford, Kansas, stated:

I have repeatedly offered $1000 to anyone who can prove to me from the Bible alone that I am bound to keep Sunday holy. There is no such law in the Bible. It is a law of the holy Catholic Church alone. The Bible says, *"Remember the Sabbath day to keep it holy."* The Catholic Church says: "No, by divine power I abolish the Sabbath day and command you to keep holy the first day of the week." And lo! The entire civilized world bows down in a reverent obedience to the command of the holy Catholic Church.[16]

Peter R. Kraemer, Catholic church Extension Society (1975), Chicago, Illinois, said the following:

Regarding the change from the observance of the Jewish Sabbath to the Christian Sunday, I wish to draw your attention to the facts:

1. That Protestants, who accept the Bible as the only rule of faith and religion, should by all means go back to the observance of the Sabbath. The fact that they do not, but on the contrary observe Sunday, stultifies them in the eyes of every thinking man.

2. We Catholics do not accept the Bible as the only rule of faith. Besides the Bible we have the living Church, the authority of the Church, as a rule to guide us. We say, this Church instituted by Christ to teach and guide man through life, has the right to change the ceremonial laws of the Old Testament, and hence, we accept her change of the Sabbath to Sunday. We frankly say, yes, the Church made this change, made this law, as she made many other laws, for instance, the Friday abstinence, the unmarried priesthood, the laws concerning mixed marriages, the regulation of Catholic marriages and a thousand other laws.

The Catholic Church changed the observance of the Sabbath to Sunday by right of the divine infallible authority given to her by Founder, Jesus Christ. The

Protestants claiming the Bible to be the only guide of faith, has no warrant for observing Sunday. In this matter the Seventh Day Adventist is the only consistent Protestant.[17]

Protestants

LUTHERAN

Martin Luther himself while it is said believed in and practiced the observance of the seventh-day Sabbath, did not prescribe it in his articles of faith for his followers, in the copies we now have access to. However, it has been said that in his original thesis Luther advocated the observance of the Sabbath, but that his colleagues objected on the grounds that it was an unpopular doctrine, which would have the tendency to repulse supporters of the reformation who were not as pious as they should have been, but were of great assistance against the usurpation of the papacy.[18]

We have seen how gradually the impression of the Jewish Sabbath faded away from the mind of the Christian church and how completely the newer thought underlying the observance of the first day took possession of the church. We have seen that Christians of the first three centuries never confused one with the other, but celebrated both.[19]

They [Roman Catholics] refer to the Sabbath day as having been changed into the Lord's Day, contrary to the

Decalogue as it seems. Neither is there an example where of they make more than concerning the changing of the Sabbath Day. Great, say they, is the power of the church, since it has dispensed with one of the Ten Commandments.[20]

But they err in teaching that Sunday has taken the place of the Old Testament Sabbath and therefore must be kept as the seventh day had to be kept by the children of Israel… These churches err in their teaching, for scripture has in no way ordained the first day of the week in place of the Sabbath. There is simply no law in the New Testament to that effect.[21]

The festival of Sunday, like all other festivals, was only a human ordinance, and it was far from the intentions of the apostles to establish a Divine command in this respect, far from them, and from the early apostolic church, to transfer the laws of the Sabbath to Sunday.[22]

ANGLICAN/EPISCOPAL

And where are we told in the scriptures that we are to keep the first day at all? We are commanded to keep the seventh; but we are nowhere commanded to keep the first day…. The reason why we keep the first day of the week holy instead of the seventh is for the same reason that we observe many other things, not because the Bible, but because the church enjoined it.[23]

We have made the change from the seventh day to the

first day, from Saturday to Sunday, on authority of the one holy Catholic Church.[24]

There is no word, no hint, in the New Testament about abstaining from work on Sunday...into the rest of Sunday; no divine law enters... The observance of Ash Wednesday or Lent stands exactly on the same footing as the observance of Sunday.[25]

Phillip Carrington (1892-1975), the Anglican archbishop of Quebec, spoke on this subject in an address to a large assembly of clergymen. It was widely reported in the news media at the time.

The Bible commandment says on the seventh day thou shall rest. That is Saturday. Nowhere in the Bible is it laid down that worship should be done on Sunday.[26]

METHODIST

But the moral law contained in the Ten Commandments, and enforced by the prophets, He Christ did not take it away. It was not the design of His coming to revoke any part of this. This is a law which can never be broken....Every part of this law must remain in force upon all mankind, and all ages; as not depending either on time or place, or any circumstances liable to change, but on the nature of God and the nature of man, and their unchangeable relation to each other.[27]

Take the matter of Sunday. There are indications in the

New Testament as to how the church came to keep the first day of the week as its day of worship, but there is no passage telling Christians to keep that day, or transfer the Jewish Sabbath to that day.[28]

The famous evangelist of his time and the founder of the Moody Bible Institute, Dwight L. Moody (1837-1889) said the following:

The Seventh Day Sabbath was binding in Eden, and it has been in force ever since. This fourth commandment begins with the word *remember*, showing that the Sabbath already existed when God wrote the law on the tables of stone at Sinai. How can men claim that this one commandment has been done away with when they will admit the other nine are still binding?[29]

This fourth is not a commandment for one place, or one time, but for all places and times.[30]

PRESBYTERIAN

The Sabbath is a part of the Decalogue-the ten commandments. This alone forever settles the question as to the perpetuity of the institution…Until, therefore, it can be shown that the moral law has been repealed, the Sabbath will stand…The teaching of Christ confirms the perpetuity of the Sabbath.[31]

Sunday being the first day of which the Gentiles [pagans] solemnly adore that planet and called it Sunday, partly from its influence on that day especially, and partly in respect to its influence on that day especially, and partly in respect to its divine body [as they conceived it] the Christians thought it fit to keep the same day and the same name of it, that they might not appear carelessly peevish, and by that means hinder the conversion of the Gentiles [pagans], and bring a greater prejudice that might be otherwise taken against the gospel.[32]

BAPTIST

Dr. Edward T. Hiscox, the author of the Baptist Manual, presented the following before a New York minister's conference on November 13, 1893:

There was and is a commandment to keep holy the Sabbath day, but that Sabbath day was not Sunday. It will be said, however, and with some show of triumph, that the Sabbath was transferred from the seventh to the first day of the week…Where can the record of such a transaction be found? Not in the New Testament absolutely not.

To me it seems unaccountable that Jesus, during the three years interaction with His disciples, often conversing with them upon the Sabbath question….never alluded to any transference of the day; also, that during forty days of His resurrection life, no such thing was intimated.

Of course, I quite well know that Sunday did come into use in early Christian history…But what a pity it comes branded with the mark of paganism, and christened with the name of the sun god, adopted by the papal apostasy, and bequeathed as a sacred legacy to Protestantism![33]

DISCIPLES OF CHRIST

"But," say some, "it was changed from the seventh to the first day." Where? When? and by whom? No man can tell. No; it never was changed, nor could it be, unless creation was to be gone through again: for the reason assigned must be changed before the observance, or respect to the reason, can be changed! It is all old wives' fables to talk of the change of the Sabbath from the seventh to the first day. If it be changed, it was that august personage changed it who changes times and laws ex officio—I think his name is Doctor Antichrist.[34]

The first day of the week is commonly called the Sabbath. This is a mistake. The Sabbath of the Bible was the day just preceding the first day of the week. The first day of the week is never called the Sabbath anywhere in the entire bible scriptures. It is also an error to talk about the change of the Sabbath from Saturday to Sunday. There is not in any place in the Bible any intimation of such a change.[35]

CONGREGATIONALISTS

...*it is quite* clear that however rigidly or devotedly we may spend Sunday, we are not keeping the Sabbath... the Sabbath was founded on a specific Divine command. We can plead no such command for the obligation to observe Sunday…There is not a single sentence in the New Testament to suggest that we incur any penalty by violating the supposed sanctity of Sunday.[36]

ORTHODOX [EASTERN]:

The ancient Christians were very careful in the observance of Saturday, or the seventh day…It is plain that all the Oriental churches, and the greatest part of the world, observed the Sabbath as a festival…Athanasius likewise tells us that they held religious assemblies on the Sabbath, not because they were infected with Judaism, but to worship Jesus, the Lord of the Sabbath, Epiphanius says the same.[37]

John Trigilio, PhD., and Kenneth Brighenti, PhD., who are both Catholic priests, say the following:

So why then do Catholic, Protestant, Orthodox Christians go to church on Sunday, treating it as the Lord's Day instead of Saturday? In general Catholicism and Christianity moved the celebration of the Lord's Day from Saturday to Sunday because Jesus rose from the dead on Easter Sunday. In other words Sunday become the Christian Sabbath, the day of rest, to honor the day Christ rose from the dead?[38]

The preceding statements show that the consensus of these church leaders and writers is that Saturday is indeed the Sabbath. It is possible that some of them did observe the Sabbath Day. I would not be surprised if many devoted Sunday preachers today are, in fact, observing the Sabbath without the knowledge of their congregants, and they use the Sabbath to fine-tune their sermons for Sunday.

I also believe that many people recognize Saturday as the Sabbath but have not actively engaged in honoring this day. However, others have acted in obedience in observing the Sabbath and exercise due diligence to the laws of God. Proverbs 15:4 and 5 states, *"That a wholesome tongue is a tree of life but perverseness therein is a breach of spirit. A fool despiseth his father's instruction but he that regardeth reproof is prudent."* Clearly there has been a breach of the everlasting covenant regarding God's holy Sabbath. However, the prophet Isaiah declared, *"… thou shall raise up the foundations of many generations; and thou shall be called, the repairer of the breach. The restorer of paths to dwell in"* (Isaiah 58:12; KJV). God is calling His people to seek out the truth and obey Him. The Sabbath is one of God's gifts to mankind, and it also foreshadows the eternal rest and expectations of the future Sabbath in the world to come.

CHAPTER SIX

SOME COMMON
DOCTRINES AND BELIEFS

T he Catholic, Protestant and various Christian denominations that worship on Sunday all seem to endorse
and practice some, if not all, of the following doctrines
and beliefs which are very common among many of today's believers. These may serve to reinforce some manmade tenets and
inaccurate interpretation of the Scriptures, including views on
the Sabbath and holy days.

1. The law is nailed to the cross.
2. Yeshua's resurrection was on Sunday; therefore, Sunday
   is the new Sabbath (the Lord's Day).
3. The observance of Ash Wednesday and the period of
   Lent
4. Yeshua, the Messiah, was crucified on Good Friday.
5. Easter instead of the Passover
6. Christmas Day, December 25, is Yeshua's birthday.
7. The promise of rest in Hebrews 4 is indicative of the new
   Sabbath (the Sabbath rest).
8. The law was a shadow of things to come.
9. There is a new covenant replacing the old.
10. Yeshua, the Messiah, fulfilled the law.
11. Observe any day.

12.   No longer under law but under grace

I have been unable to find support from a biblical perspective for some of the preceding statements. For others I have found evidence of a misguided truth. Allow me to address these common doctrines and beliefs.

The Law Is Nailed to the Cross

This statement, "the law is nailed to the cross," suggests that the law is no longer relevant, but is the seventh-day Sabbath commandment the one and only law which no longer has to be obeyed? In Colossians chapter 2, Paul focuses on a growing relationship with God through Yeshua, the Messiah. He admonishes the believers to adhere to the doctrine of Yeshua rather than to adhere to philosophy, ideas, traditions of men, and worldly principles. Colossians 2:8, *"Beware lest anyone cheat you* through philosophy and empty deceit, according to the tradition of men, according to the basic principles of the world and not according to Christ." Many churches point to the following Scripture as a reason to believe and teach that the law is irrelevant. *"having wiped out the handwriting of requirements that was against us, which was contrary to us. And He has taken it out of the way, having nailed it to the cross"* (Colossians 2:14; KJV). However, this verse refers to specific ceremonial laws and some ordinances which the Jewish council administers and holds its citizens accountable More importantly when He *"wiped away the bill of charges against us"* mentioned in Colossians 2:14; (CJB), Yeshua really nailed mankind lawlessness to the cross—not the law. A person's sin is lawlessness.

> *"And you being dead in your trespasses and the uncircumcision of your flesh, He has made alive together with Him having forgiven you all your trespasses"* (Colossians 2:13).

I find this very intriguing statement by Yeshua when He spoke to the multitudes and the disciples in Matthew 23:2, 3:

> *"The Scribes and Pharisees sit in Moses seat; therefore whatever they tell you to observe, that observe and do but do not do according to their works, for they say and do not do."*

Some 613 laws/commandments were codified as "Mosaic laws." These Mosaic laws can be divided into 365 "negative" ones—to abstain from a certain act and 248 "positive" ones—to perform a certain act. An additional seven divine or Rabbinic laws were later included, making the total 620. These laws had to do with a person's relationship with God, sacrifices, offerings, diet, priests/temple worship, sabbatical, men, women, clothing, and his status, etc. These are not the Ten Commandments per se, but rather an expansive extension of strict ordinances which also included others which were added later. Paul is vividly illustrating that the high priest no longer has to make a sin offering with the blood of animals for a person's atonement (forgiveness).

In applying the Mosaic Law under the old covenant, it was customary for the high priest to enter the temple once a year on the Day of Atonement. He would go behind the second veil (a thick curtain) into the "Holy of Holies"—into the presence of God. The high priest would sprinkle the blood of sacrificial lamb over the mercy seat under which rested the ark with the two tablets of the covenants and commandments, Aaron's rod that bore the flowering almond buds, and a pot with manna. With the sacrificial death on the cross, Yeshua, the Messiah, paid man's sin debt in full. That very moment when Yeshua gave up His Spirit, the Bible states that the veil of the temple was torn from top to bottom (See Matthew 27:50-52 and Mark 15:37, 38). This was a confirmation that taking the blood of sacrificed animal to the temple in the Holy of Holies to aid in the forgiveness of sin would no longer be necessary. Yeshua, the Messiah, was the perfect High Priest and the perfect sacrifice.

Paul continued, *"so let no one judge you in food or in drink, or regarding a festival or new moon or Sabbaths, which are a shadow of things to come, but the substance is of Christ"* (Colossians 2:17, 18). The preceding statement does not repudiate the law or suggest that it is acceptable to eat and drink what one desires and ignore the dietary laws, feast days, and the Sabbaths. Paul was telling the believers at Colosse that they should not be swayed by the criticism of unbelievers who may view their practices as ritualistic and that they should demonstrate obedience in all things to the glory of Yeshua. After all, Yeshua the Messiah is preeminent, being the first and foremost in everything; He is our sustenance. Yeshua strongly stated in Matthew 7:1 and 2, *"Judge not that you be not judged. For with what judgment you judge, you will be judged and with the measure you use, it will be measured back to you."* Participation and observance of these feast days, new moon and Sabbaths are merely a glimpse or reflection of the eternal hope and experience that awaits us, and we should never lose our focus which is Yeshua, the Messiah, and not doing what is expected of us. In Colossians 2:20-22, Paul also warns against subjecting yourself to regulations, according to the doctrine of men (self-imposed religion, false humility and even the neglect of the body).

Sunday as the Lord's Day

Sunday marks the first day of the week. The fact that Yeshua, the Messiah, was resurrected from the grave on the first day of the week now popularized as Easter Sunday in the Christian world gave credence to Sunday's being known as the "Lord's Day" and is now considered the day of worship replacing the seventh-day Sabbath. Sunday keeping was enacted by law.

The earliest recognition of the observance of Sunday as a legal duty is a constitution of Constantine in 321 A.D.; enacting that all courts of justice, inhabitants of towns and workshops were to be at rest on Sunday (venerabili die solis), with an exception of favor of those engaged in agricultural labor.[1]

No biblical evidence exists to suggest this change as neither Yeshua nor His disciples and apostles declared this. As previously mentioned, the eight references concerning the first day of the week did not mention any Sunday church services. John's reference to being in the spirit on the Lord's Day on the Isle of Patmos (Revelation 1:10) is also corroborated as a reason for Sunday worship. I firmly believe that this was on the seventh day (Saturday), the Sabbath day. Moses was called out on the Sabbath day to begin his first forty days and forty nights of communing with God (Exodus 24:16). Exodus 20:10 (KJV) clearly states *"...the sabbath of the LORD thy God...."* Isaiah 58:13 declared *"...My Holy day"* and Yeshua said, *"He is Lord of the Sabbath."*

Ash Wednesday and Lent

The celebration of Ash Wednesday marks the first day of Lent, a period of forty working days before Easter. This period of Lent is considered a time of penitence or repentance, fasting or abstinence, and even putting ashes on one's forehead as a mark of penitence. However, no mention is made of this practice in the Bible. As a matter of fact, the season of Lent began in the third century A.D. as an annual ritual of forty days fast. Pope Gregory 1 (509-604 A.D.) introduced it to the church at a time when Sunday was the beginning of Lent, and there were certain fasting days and abstinence from meats. Pope Urban II (1088-1099 A.D.) later recommended to the church that Ash Wednesday would mark the start of the celebration and the application of ashes was permissible. By this time, symbols and idol figures had already been introduced into the church.

Good Friday

The claim that Yeshua, the Messiah, was crucified on the much celebrated "Good Friday" is erroneous. As a matter of fact, there is absolutely no need for recognizing this day as proposed because Yeshua was crucified on Passover Day—not on Good Friday. The day of Passover was previously prescribed about 1,400 years earlier, prior to the departure of the Hebrews/Israelites from Egypt and to be celebrated for all time. The church either chose this day in the fourth century A.D. when it all began in error or as a deliberate attempt to be separated from the Jews.

However, there is a visible disconnect between the Jews and Gentiles as the majority of Gentile Christians accepted Good Friday (instituted by man nearly 400 years after Yeshua the Messiah's crucifixion) to celebrate the Messiah, our Passover Lamb, and yet ignore the Passover, which was designated to be celebrated as a feast.

In recent times some pastors and leaders of Protestant churches have been inviting Jewish rabbis or teachers to speak to their congregation about the Passover. Many Jews do indeed celebrate the Passover, but they steadfastly ignore Yeshua as the Messiah, the Passover Lamb except for those who practice Messianic Judaism. I believe God's intention and desire is for a "oneness" in spirit and faith based on love and obedience to His words and commands—not for the plurality of religion and denominations through the concepts and doctrines of men.

———◆———

Easter

The choice of Easter was decided by the church leaders at the Nicaean conference over 300 years after Yeshua's resurrection. They chose Easter in order not to align with or to embrace the Passover celebration which was considered as Jewish custom. In A.D. 325 at the Council of Nicaea convened by the Roman emperor Constantine, the Nicene Creed was drawn up describing the tenets of the Christian faith. The time for Easter observance was also established at this meeting by the Emperor Constantine:

> *At the council* we also consider the issue of our holiest day, Easter and it was determined by common consent that everyone, everywhere should celebrate it on one and the same day…And in the first place, it seem very unworthy for us to keep this most sacred feast following the custom of the Jews…Since we have cast away their way of calculating the date of the festival, we can assure future generations can celebrate at the same accurate time which we have kept from the first day of Passion until the present time…[2]

As a result of the council's decision, Easter and Passover celebrations do not always occur the same period every year.

In fact, *Easter* is the English translation of the name associated with the worship of pagan fertility goddesses which were a prominent form of idolatrous worship. The Easter eggs, bunnies, and other paraphernalia are all tokens of these pagan festivals reflecting fertility and sex.

According to *The Compact Bible Dictionary*:

Ashtaroth is the plural of Ashtoreth, the name of the fertility goddesses of the ancient Near East: the Babylonian Ishtar, and Greek, Astarte; in Canaan as a consort of El Baal (male). Gesenius related the name *Ashtoreth* to the Persian word *sitarah* or "star" and connects it with Venus, the goddess of love. Both female and male false gods were worshipped with lewd rites.[3]

In the Bible, this name appears as *Ashtoreth*. This manner of idol worship was a serious problem in Israel for several hundred years after they entered Canaan. Several of their kings allowed this practice to happen, which brought God's judgment against Israel. Judges 2:11-13 says that the children of Israel forsook God and served Baal and Ashtoreth. (See Judges 10:13; 1 Samuel 7:3, 4, 12:10, 31:10; 1 Kings 11:5, 33; 2 Kings 23:13.)

Christmas Day

The recognition and celebration of December 25 "Christmas Day" as Yeshua's birthday is another inaccurate claim. This day is really paralleling the birthday of the pagan sun god.

In the Roman world the Saturnalia, December 17, was a time of merrymaking and exchange of gifts. December 25 coincides with the pagan Roman festival marking the "birthday of the unconquered sun" (Natalis Solis Invicti). It is regarded also as the birth date of the Iranian mystery god Mithras, sun of righteousness.[4]

Obviously, December 25 is clearly the birthday of the sun god and not of the "Son of God"—Yeshua. The Scripture confirms the Word became flesh, and (tabernacles) with us in John 1:14. The birth of Yeshua occurred during the month of Tishri (late September/early October) around the time of the fall feasts.

A similar view is expressed in the following statement:

December 25 was the chief feast of Mithras, and in fixing on that date for Christmas, the early church sought to overlay both the Mithraic festival and Saturnalia.[5]

Mithraism pagan cult worship was prominent in the Greco-Roman world before the advent of Christianity. As a result of this cultural influence, many pagan rituals were assimilated into the early church. Some of these rituals are still evident today.

The celebration of Christmas began in the early fourth century in Rome (A.D. 336), several hundred years after Yeshua's birth, death, resurrection and ascension. It is clear that December 25 is derived from the birthday of the sun god—not the Son of God.

Is Yeshua's birthday important to you? If it is, I encourage you to carefully examine the historical and cultural origins of the current Christmas celebrations. I strongly believe and accept and would like to reiterate that Yeshua, the Messiah, was most likely born during the biblical month of Tishri (late September early October) around 5 B.C., during the fall feasts, which included the Feast of the Tabernacles—not during winter. The Scripture confirms that the Word became flesh and dwelt (tabernacled) among us. John 1:14 reads, *"and the word became flesh and dwelt among us and we beheld his glory, the glory as of the only begotten of the father full of grace and truth."* It is important to recognize that Yeshua came in the flesh as Yeshua to dwell among men. The guidance of the Holy Spirit (Rauch HaKodesh) is an awesome guide for you as you search for truth and make the connections.

Many of the festivities and rituals associated with Ash Wednesday, Lent, Easter and Christmas celebrations are largely manifestations of pagan practices which have been adapted by the church but have no biblical basis. As time marches forward and we watch and pray for Messiah's second coming, it would be wise to examine and understand the ordained appointed feasts, which will bring believers into obedience and covenant with God in preparation for the Messiah's future return and wedding feasts.

The Sabbath Rest

Over the years I have observed reference made to Hebrews chapter 4, contextually giving the idea that the seventh-day Sabbath day is no longer relevant. In Hebrews 4:1-10, the writer, in addressing the Hebrew (Jewish) Messianic believers, informs them that an eternal Sabbath rest is available to them through the Messiah. The purpose of the gospel as preached is to remind us of what we need to do or how to live our lives as well as to encourage us to ultimately seek rest for our soul.

Ezekiel 18:4 declared, *"Behold all souls are mine."* Definitely the God does not want any soul to perish. Yeshua said, *"Come to Me, all who labor and are heavy laden, and I will give you rest. Take My yoke upon you and learn from Me, for I am gentle and lowly in heart, and you will find rests for your souls."* (Matthew 11:28, 29) Yeshua is entreating nonbelievers to seek Him, learn about Him, and follow Him because it is by Him and through

Him will the ultimate rest and the blessed hope for eternity accomplished.

In Luke 10:25, a lawyer asked Yeshua what shall he do to inherit eternal life. Before responding Yeshua asked him what was written in the law. The lawyer answered, *"Thou shall love the Lord thy God with all thy heart, with all thy soul, and with all thy strength, and with all thy mind; and thy neighbor as thyself."* Yeshua responded that if he does that he shall live.

This statement is also repeated by Yeshua in response to the rich young ruler in Matthew 19:17. *"But if you want to enter life keep the commandments."* In both conversations Yeshua shows that obeying the law is a vital part in the process toward eternal life as it tells us when we sin. *"For by the law is the knowledge of sin"* (Romans 3:20).

Yeshua also points out that in the application of the law, there should be unselfish and tangible evidence in our actions. In other words, one should know the Word, apply it and live it. The lawyer needed to show mercy, and the rich man needed to be more generous. Evidently we can miss out on our salvation by focusing on who we are and what we have and lose sight of the Messiah. God has prepared this resting place from the end of His creation at the foundation of the world. Unbelief and disobedience are the only stumbling blocks that can prevent our entering God's eternal rest. According to the Scriptures in Hebrews 3:16-18, unbelief and disobedience and finally death were the outcome of the Hebrews/Israelites who rebelled during the time of the wilderness wandering.

The call is, *"Today if you will hear his voice, do not harden your hearts"* (Hebrews 3:15; Hebrews 4:7; Psalm 95:7, 8). An individual's response to God's call is the first step in the act of obe-dience. Hebrews 4:9-11 says,

> *"There remains therefore a rest for the people of God; [10]for anyone who enters God's rest also rests from his own work just as God did from his. [11]Let us therefore, make every effort to enter that rest. Lest anyone fall according to the example of disobedience."*

Entering the Sabbath rest is a great promise, and every believer is afforded the opportunity to observe and enjoy the weekly seventh day Sabbath and the other holy day Sabbaths while anticipating the eternal rest and the glorious Sabbath celebration that will be available in the future kingdom with Yeshua. (See Isaiah 66:22, 23.) One should never take for granted the writer of Hebrews conversation and suggests that observing the seventh-day Sabbath is no longer necessary. Indeed the seventh-day Sabbath is a physical day of rest commanded by God to be kept holy, to praise, to worship, and to commune with Him. It is a time to celebrate the believer's personal and spiritual rest in Him. The Sabbath is the fourth of God's commandments (law), and God's laws have not changed with the exception of the ceremonial laws and of the priestly atonement for sin with offerings and sacrifices that were replaced with the ultimate sacrifice of Yeshua, the Messiah.

The Law as a Shadow

Hebrews 10:1, *"for the law, having a shadow of the good things to come, and not the very image of the things can never with these same sacrifices, which they offer continually year by year, make those approach perfect.*" In this verse, the law refers to the ceremonial law, ordinances of animal (blood) sacrifices. Verse 4 continues, *"For it is not possible that the blood of bulls and goats could take away sins."* Animal sacrifices were insufficient as they only provided a temporary covering of human sin. Therefore, only the blood of Yeshua, the Messiah (God-incarnate in flesh), had the power to take away sin. The death of Yeshua, the Messiah, fulfills God's will and was the ultimate sacrifice and atonement once and for all time. (See also Colossians 2:17, 18.)

In Ephesians 2:11-18, the Apostle Paul states that through the death and the blood of Yeshua, the Messiah, man has been brought nearer to God. This access to Yeshua, the Messiah, has no longer made us an alien from the commonwealth of Israel and strangers from the covenant of promise, having no hope and without God in the world. Paul continued that Yeshua, the Messiah, is our peace and has broken down the wall of separation between Jews and Gentiles.

> *"Having abolished in His flesh the enmity, that is, the law of commandments contained in ordinances, so as to create in Himself one new man from the two thus making peace"* (Ephesians 2:15).

Peter's vision in Acts 10:9-16 further confirmed that the message of salvation must be taken to the Gentiles or to the nations as the wall of separation was removed. This confirmation is contrary to the belief that this vision annulled the dietary laws recorded in Leviticus 11 and Deuteronomy 14. Therefore, it is acceptable to eat pork, bacon, shrimp, lobster, catfish, etc.

Yeshua, the Messiah's death and His shed blood removed the enmity and separation once created by the ordinances of ceremonial laws, circumcision, animal sacrifices and offerings in order to reconcile all to God by way of the cross.

These sacrificial laws were really only a shadow (a reflection) to God's ultimate gift to His Son Yeshua and the great promise of eternal life. These laws are separate and apart from the Ten Commandments, which are a binding contract instructing man how to live.

The New Covenant

In addition to the Ten Commandments, the law of covenants was also given to Moses. Also included in this covenant was the command that the people should worship no other God because He was a jealous God. They should make no idols. They should observe the Sabbath, work only six days and rest on the seventh. They should observe all yearly/annual feasts. The covenant was broken during Moses' first 40 days/40 nights commune with God on Mt. Sinai when the people gave some of their golden earrings to Aaron to create the golden calf idol which the people worshipped (Exodus 32:1-6). God, however, renewed the covenant with some consequences.

In Deuteronomy 29:1, God commanded Moses to establish another covenant with the Hebrews/Israelites while they were living in Moab. The details of the covenant were outlined at a general assembly of all Israel. Moses said,

> *"Therefore keep the words of the covenant, and do them, that you may prosper in all that you do. All of you stand*

today before the LORD your God: your leaders and your tribes, and your elders and your officers, all the men of Israel, your little ones and your wives—also the stranger who is in your camp, from the one who cuts your wood to the one who draws your water; that you may enter into covenant with the LORD your God and into His oath, which the LORD your God makes with you today, that He may establish you as a people for Himself, and that He may be God to you, just as He has sworn to you, and just as He has sworn to your fathers, to Abraham, Isaac, and Jacob." I make this covenant and this oath, not with you alone, but with him who stands here with us today before the LORD our God, as well as with him who is not here with us today" (Deuteronomy 29:9-14).

Moses explained the promise of blessings for obedience to the covenant and further warned the children of Israel of consequences for violating them. In the end, God will change their hearts and remove the vile, stubbornness and rejection that exists toward God. Deuteronomy 30:6 says,

"And the LORD your God will circumcise your heart and the heart of your descendants, to love the LORD your God with all your heart and with all your soul, that you may live."

The covenant was made not only with those present, but it was also for all future generations.

Several years later during the reign of King Josiah, Jeremiah the prophet lamented and utterly warned the children of Judah of their rejection and disobedience to God. They had broken their covenant with God by worshipping and participating in many acts of idolatry. Jeremiah 31:31-33 tells of God's promise of a new covenant that would be written in their hearts. It is interesting to note that during the time of Jeremiah, the people of the southern kingdom (Judah) were taken into Babylonian captivity, which lasted for a period of 70 years.

In addressing the Jewish believers in Yeshua, the Messiah, in Hebrews 8:7-13, Paul made direct reference to the words written by Jeremiah regarding the covenant. Hebrews 9:1 specifies that the first/old covenant had ordinances of divine service and earthly sanctuary, meaning that the high priest acted as mediator for himself and the people. Offerings of gifts and sacrifices were given. *"Concerned only with food, drinks, various washings, and fleshly animal ordinances imposed until the time of reformation"* (Hebrews 9:10). The focal issue in reference to the covenant is dealing specifically with the gift offerings and sacrifices. A great deal of this was done during the yearly feast observance. (See Leviticus 23.) The priests and Levites performed major roles during this time. The high priest was responsible to enter the inner chambers of the temple/tabernacle with the animal blood to seek atonement for the sins of the people. There were limitations to this earthly service; therefore, Yeshua, the Messiah, came as man's High Priest.

"And for this reason He is the mediator of the new covenant, by means of death for the redemption of the transgression under the first covenant, that those who are called may receive the promise of the eternal inheritance" (Hebrews 9:15).

———◆———

Yeshua, the Messiah, was offered once to bear the sins of all, thus fulfilling God's will. Once you have answered the call of God, that new covenant is embedded in your heart and you have made your earnest deposit to your eternal inheritance which re-quires your continual obedience and allegiance to God. This new covenant did not state that the commandments were eliminated or the seventh-day Sabbath was obsolete. Ezekiel's prophecy also validated this new covenant.

> "I will give you a new heart and put a new spirit in you; I will remove from you a heart of stone and give you a heart of flesh. And I will put my spirit in you and move you to follow my decrees and be careful to keep my laws" (Ezekiel 36:26, 27; NIV).

> The old covenant was ratified by the blood of animals (Exodus 24:5-8 and Hebrews 9: 19, 20) based upon the promises of the people that they would keep God's law. The new covenant is based on God's promise to write His law in our hearts and it was ratified with the blood of Christ (Hebrews 8:10 and Jeremiah 31:33-34).[6]

At the Passover meal with the disciples, Yeshua took the cup of wine and said, *"For this is my blood which ratifies the new covenant, My blood shed on behalf of many, so that they may have their sins forgiven."* (Matthew 26:28; CJB).

Matthew chapter 5 records Yeshua's sermon on the Moun-tain. In one of His statements in verse 17, Yeshua said, *"Do not think that I come to destroy the law but to fulfill."* Yeshua made it very clear that He did not come to get rid of the law but to obey and satisfy it and unveil the truths of the Scriptures. In other words, He came to further establish and confirm the law/commandments. Yeshua attended the synagogue and read from the Torah on the Sabbath. When reading verses 18 and 19, the Bible reveals the full context of what Yeshua had to say, yet this is one of the most prevalent statements to which believers give credence and use to justify that the seventh-day Sabbath is no longer necessary. More than likely, their reasoning for such a conclusion is because they have not read the rest of these verses.

Observe Any Day

"One person esteems one day above another, another esteems every day alike. Let each be fully convinced in his own mind. He who observes a day, observes it to the Lord; and he who does not observe the day, to the Lord he does not observe it" (Romans 14:5, 6).

Some believers have assumed from these verses that it is acceptable to simply observe any day; therefore, the seventh-day Sabbath is not applicable. Paul was addressing the church in Rome which consisted of both Jews and Gentiles, and some conflicts and misunderstandings regarding such issues as the proper foods to eat, fasting, etc., which had arisen. (Please read Matthew 5:17-20.) Paul refuses to get caught up in their disputes because he knew 1) They knew the law, and 2) Some issues are simply not worth debating. Therefore, he left the decision up to them as an illustration of the law of liberty. In verse 5, Paul stated, *"...Let each be fully convinced in his own mind,"* which solidifies the fact that the heart is ultimately what condemns and accepts, and God looks at the heart. Consequently, everything a Christian or believer does should honor the Messiah/Savior.

Paul sums up this entire issue in verses 10 through 13: *"For we all shall stand before the judgment seat of Yeshua-Messiah… [12]So then each of us shall give account of himself to God."* These verses clearly show that every person is responsible for his own choices but will be accountable to God the final adjudicator and rewarder. (See also 2 Corinthians 5:10.) So any idea that Paul's statement declared that the seventh-day Sabbath is no longer relevant and that man can choose to observe any day as the Sabbath is a world view; it is not biblical. At no time in the Scriptures did Paul declare himself as God or as Yeshua, the Creator and giver of all things including the law.

As a believer and follower of Messiah, we should never be confused and believe that Paul had such authority to change the Sabbath day to Sunday or to any other day. However, I see nothing wrong in worshipping on any day of the week, but that day should never be constituted as a substitute for God's prescribed holy, sanctified Sabbath day.

Interestingly, Paul begins the letter to the Romans talking about the importance of obedience to the faith as noted in 1:5 and concludes it in similar fashion in 16:26. Paul has also made it clear in I Corinthians 11:1 that we should imitate him as he imitated Yeshua-Messiah. Yeshua, Paul and all of the disciples and apostles observed the Sabbath (the fourth commandment). Observing the Sabbath is an act of obedience and compliance with the other nine commandments. The first four commandments dictate the true love, respect and honor to be displayed to a Holy God, and the remaining six tell us how to treat our parents and other people.

◆

Not Under the Law but Under Grace

This statement "not under law but under grace" is very popular among some New Testament believers. What is *grace*? *Webster's Dictionary* defines *grace* as "the love and favor of God." Significantly, grace was available from the beginning of time and long before the laws and commandments were written by God and given to Moses.

Genesis 6:8 states, *"But Noah found grace in the sight of the LORD."* Consequently God gave Noah the assignment to save his household as well as selected animal species from the disastrous flood and to become the progenitor for the world to come—the one in which we now live. Also in Exodus 33:17-19, the following disclosure can be noted:

> And the LORD said unto Moses, *"I will do this thing also that thou has spoken: for thou has found grace in my sight, and I know thee by name." And he said, "I beseech thee, shew me thy glory." And He said, "I will make all my goodness pass before thee and I will proclaim the name of the LORD before thee: and I will be gracious to whom I will be gracious and I will shew mercy on whom I will show mercy."*

Following this private discourse, Moses was summoned again to Mt. Sinai to receive the second set of two tablets of the renewed covenants and commandments as a replacement for the first set that had been broken by Moses. Moses spent another 40 days and 40 nights on the mount with God and was given the penultimate leadership assignment of the wilderness journey and governing the people unto their arrival in Canaan. The

———◆———

Psalmist also declared, *"For the* LORD *is a sun and shield: the* LORD *will give grace and glory: no good thing will He uphold from them that walk uprightly"* (Psalm 84:11).

Romans 6:14-15 contains the popular statement: *"For sin shall not have dominion over you; for ye are not under law, but under grace. What then? Shall we sin, because we are not under the law but under grace? God forbid."* Paul's statement in his letter to the Romans centered on the law and sin. The question is "what law was Paul talking about"?

Prior to this statement in Romans 5, Paul emphasized the point that salvation comes through Yeshua, the Messiah, and verse 11 reads, *"And not only so, but we also joy in God through our Lord Jesus Christ by whom we now received the atonement."* The atonement of sin or reconciliation with Yeshua was made possible through His shed blood, death and resurrection. Therefore the law of atonement which was being exercised by the high priest with the blood of animal sacrifices was no longer necessary. This is the law to which Paul was referring. To confirm more about the law and sin, verse 13 continues, *"For until the law sin was in the world, but sin was not imputed when there is no law."* Paul was now emphasizing the fact that sin existed in the world before there was any law, but nothing was attributed to or classified as sin when there was no law.

In Romans 7:7, Paul continues,

"What shall we say then? Is the law sin? God forbid. Nay I had not known sin, but by the law; for I had not known lust except the law had said, Thou shall not covet."

In verse 12, Paul made very clear the existence and the importance of the law when he added, *"Wherefore the law is holy, and the commandment holy, and just and good."* Paul concluded the chapter in verse 25 by saying,

> *"I thank God through Yeshua-Messiah our Lord. So then, with the mind I myself serve the law of God; but with the flesh the law of sin."*

Our salvation comes through the *grace* of God ("the unmerited or undeserving favor") which is a gift based on His mercy, truth and righteousness. *"For by grace are ye saved through faith; and that not of yourselves: it is the gift of God. Not of works, lest any man should boast"* (Ephesians 2:8). However, it is through belief, acknowledgment and repentance that we receive His forgiveness.

Paul has made several references in contrasting grace with the law. (See Romans 4:16; 5:20; 6:14, 15; Galatians 2:21; 5:4.) He was very careful in stating clearly that grace does not repudiate or nullify the requirements of God's law. Grace enables us to fulfill the righteousness of the law, and it does not annul the righteousness demands of the law, but it confirms and validates them (Romans 2:13, 3:31).

Grace is not a New Testament (B'rit Chadasha) phenomenon. The Bible is loaded with Scriptures pertaining to the law and grace, but let us never forget that God's laws and commandments are an everlasting covenant and we should make every effort to understand, to be equipped and to be obedient to God's instructions. As Peter admonishes us, *"But grow in grace and the knowledge of our Lord and Savior Yeshua-Messiah. To Him be Glory now and forever"* (2 Peter 3:18).

CHAPTER SEVEN

SCRIPTURAL REFERENCES ABOUT GOD'S LAWS AND COMMANDMENTS

T he countries of the world have patterned many significant laws from the Ten Commandments and have also
instituted many ordinances which are contrary to the
laws of God.

The following Old Testament (Tanakh) Scriptures, which
clearly specify the significance of the laws and commandments
of God, show truth and also express warnings and benefits.

Deuteronomy 4:2

"Ye shall not add unto the word which I command you, neither shall ye diminish ought from it, that ye may keep the commandments of the LORD your God which I command you."

Deuteronomy 4:12, 13

*"And the LORD spake unto you out of the midst of the fire ye
heard the voice of the words, but saw no similtitude; only ye
heard a voice. And he declared unto you his covenant, which
commanded you to perform, even ten commandments; and
he wrote them upon two tablets of stone."*

Deuteronomy 6:17

"You shall diligently keep the commandments of the Lord your God. His testimonies and His statutes which He has commanded you."

Deuteronomy 8:6

"therefore you shall keep the commandments of the Lord your God, to walk in his ways and to fear him."

Deuteronomy 8:11

"Beware that you do not forget the Lord your God by not keeping His commandments, His judgments, and His statutes, which I commanded to you today."

Psalm 89:34

"My covenant will I not break or alter the thing that is gone out of my lips."

Psalm 103:17, 18

"But the mercy of the Lord is from everlasting to everlasting on those who fear him, and his righteousness to children's children. To such as keep his covenant. And to those who remember his commandments to do them."

Psalm 111:9

"He sent redemption to his people: He hath commanded His covenant forever: holy and reverend is His name."

Psalm 112:1

"Praise ye the Lord, Blessed is the man that feareth the Lord that delighteth greatly in His commandments."

Psalm 119:33-35

"Teach me, O LORD *the way of Your statutes, and I shall keep it to the end. Give me understanding and I shall keep your law; indeed I will observe it with my whole heart. Make me walk in the path of Your commandments, for I delight in it."*

Psalm 119:86

"All my commandments are faithful...."

Psalm 119:142

"Your righteousness is an everlasting righteousness, and your law is truth."

Psalm 119:151

"You are near O LORD *and all your commandments are truth."*

Psalm 119:155

"Salvation is far from the wicked, for they do not seek your statutes."

Psalm 119:160

"The entirety of your word is truth and every one of your righteous judgments endures forever."

Psalm 119:165

"Great peace has those who love your law, and nothing causes them to stumble."

Proverbs 3:1

"My son forget not my law: but let thine heart keep my commandments."

Proverbs 6:23

"For the commandment is a lamp; and the law a light; re-proofs of instruction are the way of life."

Ecclesiastes 12:13, 14

"Let us hear the conclusion of the whole matter; Fear God and keep his commandments: for this is the whole duty of man. For God will bring every work into judgment, with every secret thing whether it be good or whether it be evil."

Isaiah 48:8

"Oh that you had heeded My commandments! Then your peace would be like a river, and your righteousness like the waves of the sea."

Malachi 4:4

"Remember ye the Law of Moses my servant, which I commanded unto to him in Horeb for all Israel, with the statues and judgments."

By looking at the subsequent New Testament (B'rit Chadasha) texts, the believer can see how important it is to abide by God's instructions and what danger lurks ahead when he defers from doing so.

Both Matthew and Luke 4:4 relate Yeshua's being tempted by the devil for 40 days and 40 nights. In verse 3, the devil told Yeshua that if He was the Son of God, He should command that the stones become bread.

Yeshua answered, *"It is written man shall not live by bread alone but by every word that proceeds from the mouth of God."* Yeshua was simple reminding the devil who He is and, at the same time, He was referencing the parallel Scriptures in Deuteronomy 8:3.

In 2 Timothy 3:16 and 17, Paul stated, *"All scripture is given by inspiration of God and is profitable for doctrine, for reproof, for correction, for instruction in righteousness, that the man of God may be complete, thoroughly equipped for every good work."*

At the Feast of Dedication (the Festival of Lights, or Hannukah) in Jerusalem (John 10:22-28), a dialogue ensued between Yeshua and the Jews. As Yeshua entered the temple via Solomon's Porch adjoining the Court of the Gentiles, the Jews questioned Him about being the Messiah. He responded, *" I told you, and you do not believe. The works that I do in my Father's name, they bear witness of Me. But you do not believe because you are not of my sheep, as I said to you. My sheep hear my voice and I know them because they follow me."* As Yeshua continued the conversation, He expressed the unity between God and Himself as He had emphasized when He said *"I and My Father are one"* (John 10:30).

In John 10:35 Yeshua told them that the Scriptures cannot be broken. The winter Feast of Dedication memorializes the rededication of the Jerusalem temple after Judas Maccabeus and his band of men, including his sons, recaptured the city from the Syrians under Antiochus IV Epiphanes, who had polluted and desecrated the temple. It is a significant celebratory feast because the posterity of the tribe of Judah, the lineage of Yeshua the Messiah, was preserved. Yeshua used the occasion of the feast to speak to unbelievers and to point out His deity. He is indeed the light of the world.

Matthew 7:21-23 contains a serious warning: *"Not everyone*

who says to me Lord, Lord, shall enter the kingdom of heaven. Many will say to me on that day, Lord have I not prophesied in your name, cast out demons in your name, and done wonders in your name? And then I will declare to them I never knew you: depart from me you who practice lawlessness."

In Mark 7 the Pharisees are having a conversation with Yeshua about the disciples' defiling their bread by eating with dirty hands. Verses 6 through 9 (NKJV) contain the concluding statement by Yeshua as it is written:

"This people honors me with their lips but their heart is far from me. And in vain do they worship me, teaching as doctrines the commandments of men For laying aside the commandment of God you hold the tradition of men.... All too well you reject the commandment of God, that you may keep your tradition." (See also Matthew 15:9; Isaiah 29:13.)

This statement by Yeshua is true even today as many of God's Holy days have been replaced by man-created holidays and packed with the traditions of commercialism, ceremonies and rituals which are especially visible during Good Friday, Easter and Christmas celebrations.

In concluding His sermon on the plain to the great multitude who came to hear and to be healed, Yeshua spoke these words: *"but why do you call me Lord, Lord, and not do the things which I say?"* (Luke 6:46) With regard to this question, Yeshua gave a comparison between hearers and doers of His Word. In explaining one who hears and does according to His words, he said:

"He is like a man building a house, who dug deep and laid the foundation on the rock. And when the flood arose, the stream beat vehemently against the house, and could not shake it, for it was founded on a rock. But he who hears and did nothing is like a man who built a house on the earth without a foundation, against which the stream beat vehemently; and immediately it fell, and ruin of that house was great" (Luke 6:48, 49).

Yeshua was making it clear that trying to show honor while being disobedient and not acting on His words is simply—not prudent and will bring ruin.

During the last days before Yeshua's crucifixion in Jerusalem, and while He gave several exhortations, He recognized the fact that many believed in Him but would not confess Him because they feared the Pharisees. Hence in John 12:43, He responded, *"For they love the praise of men more than the praise of God."* John went on to record Yeshua's words in verse 48, *"He who rejects me and do not receive my words, has that which judges him—the word which I have spoken will judge him in the last day."* Paul also made it clear in Romans 14:11 and 12:

"For it is written, As I live says the Lord, Every knee shall bow to me. And every tongue shall confess to God. ¹²So then each of us shall give account of himself to God."

Peter, who spoke about the wisdom of Paul and exhorted the believers to be steadfast in their salvation, had the following to say:

"As also in all his epistles, speaking in them of these things, in which some are hard to understand, which untaught and unstable people twist to their own destruction, as they do also the rest of the scriptures. [17] Ye therefore beloved, seeing ye know these things before, beware lest ye also, being led away with the error of the wicked [lawless] fall from your own steadfastness" (2 Peter 3:16, 17).

The Apostle Peter shows that some of God's words declared by Paul might not be easy to understand, but there is great danger in manipulating the Scriptures.

John, the only disciple who was not martyred, lived to a ripe-old age in his nineties. During his prophecy on the Isle of Patmos mentioned in Revelation 14:12 and 13, he said,

Here is the patience of the saints, here are they that keep the commandments of God, and the faith of Yeshua. [13] Then I heard a voice from heaven saying to me, "Write: Blessed are the dead who die in the Lord from now on." "Yes" says the spirit, that they may rest from their labors, and their works follow them.

In Revelation 22:18 and 19, John also gave a strong warning against those who add or take away from the Word of God. A very similar statement was made through Moses in two places in Deuteronomy 4:2 and 12:32 as well as one by King Solomon in Proverbs 30:5 and 6.

CHAPTER EIGHT

SIGNIFICANT FEASTS, SABBATHS AND HOLY DAYS

T he following are the Feasts and Sabbath days as high-lighted in Leviticus 23, Numbers 28 and 29 and also mentioned in other Scriptures.

1. Weekly seventh-day Sabbath (Friday evening sunset to Saturday evening sunset)

2. Passover begins at sunset on the evening of the fourteenth day of the first month Abib (now Nisan) the beginning of the Biblical calendar. (See appendix C.)

3. The Feast of Unleavened Bread, a seven-day feast, begins at sunset the evening on the fifteenth day of the first month—Abib (now Nisan). The first and seventh days are Sabbath days. Abib (now Nisan) 15—the first day—is a high Sabbath (Chag-Hamatzoh). It is a holy day with holy convocation and gathering at the tabernacle.

4. The Feast of First Fruits is recognized on a specific day during the week of Passover/Feast of Unleavened Bread. (Bring a sheaf of the first fruits to the Lord. The priest waves the sheaf offering.) These holy feasts are celebrated during the month of March or April, which is the beginning of the biblical sacred calendar.

5. The Feast of Weeks/Harvest/Shavuot/Pentecost is marked

by seven full weeks or seven Sabbaths after the day of First Fruits. This feast is celebrated on the fiftieth day after the seven Sabbaths after Passover. This high Sabbath is a holy day; there should be no work and an offering should be brought to the Lord. This feast usually occurs during late May or early June.

6.   The Feast of Trumpets (Yom Teruah/Day of Shouting) begins on the first day of the seventh month (Tishri) with the blowing of trumpets. It is also known as Rosha-shana, or Jewish New Year. This is a Sabbath day. (The month of Tishri marks the beginning of the civil year on the Jewish calendar (September-October). (See Appendix D.)

7.   The Day of Atonement (Yom Kippur), which is on the tenth day of the seventh month (Tishri), is a day of holy convocation and a Sabbath of solemn rest. It is a day of corporate worship and for nations to repent. God is calling His people to repentance and to honor Him.

8.   The Feast of Tabernacles (Sukkot), a seven-day feast, begins on the fifteenth day of seventh month (Tishri). The first day is a high Sabbath—a holy day and no work. The Feast of Tabernacles takes place fifteen days from the Feast of Trumpets (Yom Teruah) or five days after Yom Kippur. On the eighth day is a Sabbath of sacred assembly (Shemini-Atzeret) known as the Last Great Day. The Feast of Tabernacles is the same as the Feast of Ingathering/Feast of Booths—a reminder of when the Hebrew or Israelites dwelt in booths and relied on God for everything. It also points to and instructs about a future time when Yeshua will tabernacle with His people again.

These Feast days and Sabbath Days are not merely for the Jews or Hebrews/Israelites to honor and obey God—the one true and living God. They are part and parcel of God's plans and commands for all people and as followers of Yeshua, we are expected to celebrate them.

THE SEVENTH DAY SABBATH

The seventh-day Sabbath is not just Saturday as we know it to be. The Sabbath begins Friday evening at sunset and ends Saturday evening at sunset—a full 24 hours. Preparation both physically and mentally should be made for the Sabbath as there should be no work including cooking or kindling of fire (Exodus 35:3) on the Sabbath day. One should also guard his tongue. James, Yeshua's brother, warned, *"And the tongue is a fire"* (James 3:6). Therefore, do not let any anger or bitterness and unwholesome thing come out of your mouth. The Sabbath is a period of refreshing, thanksgiving, prayer, praise, honor,

Yeshua at the Last Supper

Bible study, fellowship with family and friends and a time of spiritual communication with Father God through Yeshua-Messiah at home or at the church or the synagogue. Some time can also be spent visually enjoying the sights, sounds and the splendor of God's creation.

It is important to welcome the Sabbath on Friday at evening and close out the Sabbath on Saturday evening because it is a consecrated and a Holy Day set apart from the others. Seven holy Sabbath days are included in the spring and autumn (fall) feast days, and some of these holy Sabbath days may or may not fall on Saturday, the regular Sabbath day.

THE PASSOVER

The Passover originated from the time following the last plague that afflicted the Egyptian people. This celebration gives God's people an opportunity to remember the exodus from Egypt as well as the time when God allowed the death angel to pass over the Hebrews/Israelites' dwellings. In obedience, they smeared the blood of sacrificial animals on their doorposts so that the lives of their firstborn would be spared. A covenant was established between God and His people symbolized by the blood of slain animals being used as a ceremonial act of forgiveness. The Passover was the last meeting Yeshua had with His disciples before His crucifixion. On that evening as Yeshua celebrated the Passover meal with the disciples, Yeshua demonstrated that He would be the Passover lamb, and His shed blood would seal the new covenant for the forgiveness of sins. Matthew 26:17-30, relates Yeshua's conversation with the disciples prior to, during, and after the Passover meal.

"...the disciples came to Jesus, saying unto him, Where wilt thou that we prepare for thee to eat the passover? [18]And he said, Go into the city to such a man, and say unto him, The Master saith, My time is at hand; I will keep the passover at thy house with my disciples. [19]And the disciples did as Jesus had appointed them; and they made ready the passover....[26]And as they were eating, Jesus took bread, and blessed it, and brake it, and gave it to the disciples, and said, Take, eat; this is my body. [27]And he took the cup, and gave thanks, and gave it to them, saying, Drink ye all of it; [28]For this is my blood of the new testament, which is shed for many for the remission of sins. [29]But I say unto you, I will not drink henceforth of this fruit of the vine, until that day when I drink it new with you in my Father's kingdom" (Matthew 26:17-29; KJV).

(See also Mark 14:12-26; Luke 22:7-20; 1 Corinthians 11:23-30.)

Significantly Yeshua was crucified on Passover day Wednesday, Abib/Nisan 14, A.D. 30 as the Lamb of God (John 1:29) and our Passover (1 Corinthians. 5:7, 8). No bone of the lamb must be broken (Exodus 12:46), and none of Yeshua's bones were broken. The following day (Thursday), being the first day of the Feast of Unleavened Bread, was a high Sabbath Day. John 19:31 and 42 state:

"Therefore because it was preparation day the bodies should not remain on the cross on the Sabbath day (for that Sabbath day was a high day) the body of Yeshua was buried before sunset by Joseph of Arimathea and Nicodemus, two

of Yeshua's believers who were members of the Jewish council....⁴²So there they laid Yeshua because of the Jews' preparation day, for the tomb was nearby."

Yeshua was crucified and buried on Wednesday (Passover day) before sunset, the start of Thursday's high holy Sabbath, which was the first day of the Feast of Unleavened Bread—and Saturday's being the regular Sabbath. Yeshua was therefore not crucified on Friday as many have been led to believe.

Yeshua rose from the grave sometime after sunset on Saturday evening which begins the first day of the week (night is the dark part of the day) and fulfilling the very words He spoke in Matthew 12:40, which says, *"For as Jonah was three days and three nights in the belly of the great fish, so will the Son of man be three days and three nights in the heart of the earth."* Let's check it: Yeshua was in the grave Wednesday night, Thursday (day), Thursday night, Friday (day), Friday night, and Saturday (day), and He rose Saturday night which is already Sunday, the first day of the week. Yeshua was in the grave precisely three days and three nights as He had said.

A Friday crucifixion would mean that Yeshua was in the grave Friday night, Saturday (day) and Saturday night—roughly 36 hours, representing one day and two nights—only half the period of time that Yeshua revealed to the scribes and Pharisees. A new day begins at evening at sunset and ends at sunset the following day—not from 12:01 a.m. (night) one day to 12 midnight the next day as we have been taught and led to believe. Rather, a day begins and ends at sunset, a full twenty-four-hour cycle representing twelve night hours from sunset to sunrise and twelve day hours from sunrise to sunset. (Mark 1:32 and Luke 4:40 describe a period of a day when Yeshua performed healing after sunset at the end of Sabbath.) Yeshua's fulfillment of the Passover being the sacrificial Lamb has enhanced its significance, and the Passover will continue to be memorialized as an annual event of great spiritual meaning.

The Passover and the Feast of Unleavened Bread are celebrated over a period of eight days. The first day marked the day when the Passover meal is eaten as well as the day when the sacrificial animals were usually slaughtered. The meal commemorates the time when the death angel "passed over" the dwellings of the Hebrews/Israelites and saved all of the first born prior to their exodus from Egypt and freedom from the bondage and slavery as previously discussed.

———◆———

THE FEAST OF UNLEAVENED BREAD

The Feast of Unleavened Bread begins the day following the Passover day and lasts for seven days when the unleavened bread is eaten. The first and seventh days are Sabbath days. The first day is regarded as a high Sabbath, and gathering (Holy convocation) at the synagogue or church is required for males. Yeshua became the Passover Lamb—the ultimate sacrifice for man's sins. The unleavened bread without additives represents Yeshua as pure and as the Bread of life. He was without sin, and His body did not see corruption (Psalm 16:10). He was sanctified and set apart.

THE FEAST OF FIRST FRUITS

The Feast of First Fruits is the day during the Passover/Feast of Unleavened Bread when the daily count begins, toward the Feast of Shavout/Pentecost. This is usually a day when an offering of the first fruits of harvest or a monetary offering is brought to the Lord.

Some religious and Jewish communities regard the second day of Passover/Feast of Unleavened Bread (the day of the high Sabbath) as the day to begin counting the 49 days of Omer, a period known as the Feast of Weeks and concludes on the fiftieth day with the celebration of Shavuot/Pentecost. The Christian communities use Easter Sunday (Resurrection Sunday)—a fixed date as the first day in counting the days leading to the Day of Pentecost. For this reason, Pentecost always falls on Sunday. Although there may be difference in opinion in determining the day of First Fruits when counting the days of Omer, the Scripture reveals that Yeshua represents the First Fruit. He was the first to be resurrected from the grave and to eternity or eternal life (1 Corinthians 15:20, 23).

THE FEAST OF WEEKS/HARVEST/SHAVOUT /PENTECOST

The Feast of Weeks/Harvest usually marked the beginning of the barley harvest leading up to the celebration of Shavuot/ Pentecost. Traditionally, the farmers in Israel brought the first of their crops *bikkurim* to Jerusalem in a joyful procession of thanksgiving, ending at the temple mount. Shavout/Pentecost is fifty days from the day of First Fruits (the day of Yeshua's resurrection). Seven weeks or seven Sabbaths are counted from the day of first fruits—the day after the Sabbath which is 49 days plus 1, totaling 50 days (Leviticus 23:15-17).

Pentecost is derived from the Greek word *Pente-koste* (Hemera) meaning "the fiftieth day." It is one of God's appointed holy days to be celebrated annually. The Christian community is well aware of the relevance of Pentecost, but how many churches/believers celebrate this significant and eventful feast? This one-day feast, culminating the feast of weeks, represents the end of the wheat/grain harvest.

After His resurrection, Yeshua, the Messiah, spent forty days (Acts 1:3) on earth before His ascension to His Father, and ten days later at 9:00 a.m. while the disciples and many believers assembled in Jerusalem, the promised Comforter or Holy Spirit descended on them (John 14:16, 17), thus culminating the fifty days. They all witnessed and embraced this outpouring of the Holy Spirit. (See Acts 2:1-4.)

This event occurring on the day of Shavuot/Pentecost represents the new covenant and advent of the new church age. It also symbolizes the circumcision of the heart and conviction of believers by the Holy Spirit, by grace and truth through faith in Yeshua, the Messiah, and the beginning harvest of many who will be in the first resurrection (Revelation 20:6). It is considered also a memorial of the day and time Moses received the Torah, the commandments and laws at Mount Sinai (Exodus 19; 24:12-18). These two phenomenal events took place on an early spring morning with very similar sights and sounds as the power of God unfolded.

One event took place at Mt. Sinai and the other at Mt. Zion (Jerusalem). About 3,000 souls perished in the camp at Mt. Sinai because they had forsaken God's command by worshipping the idol of the golden calf (Exodus 32:25-30). Three thousand souls were saved at Mt. Zion following the acceptance of the Holy Spirit (Acts 2:40). These spring feasts and events have all been fulfilled by Yeshua.

THE FEAST OF TRUMPETS OR NEW MOON

The Feast of Trumpets (Yom Teruah) or New Moon, the only feast that falls on a new moon, is marked by the blowing of trumpets (the shofar or the ram's horn) and is also the start of the Jewish civil year (New Year) or Rosh Hashanah. Significantly, the Feast of Trumpets is not simply a celebration but is a reminder to seek repentance and forgiveness and to prepare us to welcome the Yeshua, the Messiah's promised return as King. It foreshadows Yeshua's final call for the remnants of Israel and others to repent and to obey Him. Yeshua, the Messiah, came as our High Priest and made remission for our sins by His shed blood at Calvary, and He will return as King of kings and Lord of lords at the upcoming judgment.

THE DAY OF ATONEMENT

The Day of Atonement is a Sabbath day of solemn rest and fasting. Leviticus 16 details the ceremonial process conducted by the high priest. The high priest was a foreshadowing of Yeshua, the Messiah, our High Priest (Hebrews 8:1-6 and 9:22-24). The Day of Atonement also pictures those who will be saved at the future coming judgment after the return of Yeshua, the Messiah, as King. It gives us the opportunity to seek repentance individually and corporately as a nation.

THE FEAST OF TABERNACLES/INGATHERING

The Feast of Tabernacles/Ingathering (Sukk'ot or Booths) commemorate the Hebrews'/Israelites' entrance into the Promised Land after God kept them forty years in the wilderness. This last of the feasts prescribed by God highlights the Hebrews'/Israelites' experience during the pilgrimage from Egypt. The first day is a high Sabbath, and the eighth day, which is also a Sabbath, is called the Last Great Day. According to the prophet Malachi, the prophet Elijah will return in an attempt to reconcile the remnants of Israel. This feast symbolizes the future kingdom age of the New Millennium when Satan will be bound for a thousand years, and the resurrected saints will be living and reigning with Yeshua as explained in Revelation Chapter 20.

The first four feasts which occur in the season of spring foreshadow the events in the life of Yeshua that were ordained over 1,400 years before Yeshua the Messiah came. These feasts were all fulfilled with the coming of Yeshua, the Messiah. However, believers should continue to celebrate them as a memorial. They were appointed by God.

The last three celebrations in autumn, classified as "Fall Feasts" represent the holiest period on the Jewish calendar and include four special holy Sabbath days in addition to the regular weekly seventh-day Sabbath. These holy days symbolize prophetic events which are prophesied both in the Old and New Testaments (Tanakh and B'rit-Chadasha). The Scriptures made it available for everyone to see and have an understanding. These appointed feasts, which occur during the fall, depict future events associated with Yeshua's second coming.

Without any reservation, I regard these feasts as being mandatory for all followers of Yeshua to celebrate. These feasts are not simply for the Jews or Hebrews/Israelites to celebrate because all Gentile believers also worship the same one true and Living God and are grafted in as spiritual Israelites. Importantly, these are God's feasts and are special appointments that He made with His people.

These feasts represent the prophetic fulfillment of events regarding Yeshua, the Messiah, and are a precursor of events to come. Strangely though, these feasts are celebrated mainly by the Jewish people who have followed the Torah and a small quantity of the world's population who recognize their significance.

> The people of the world today are ignorant of God's holy days and do not keep them. Therefore they have no comprehension of the events they foreshadow.[1]

Believers and followers of Yeshua should recognize, honor

and celebrate God's Holy Days with great fervor and vibrancy because these Holy days have greater meaning and importance than the holidays instituted by man. Yeshua observed all of the Sabbaths and feasts during His earthly sojourn. Luke 2:42 recorded Yeshua's first public discourse at the age of twelve following the Passover that He had attended in Jerusalem. John 2:13-16 also revealed Yeshua's visit to the temple a few days before another Passover when He drove out the money changers and sellers who were conducting business at the temple.

John 6:4-14 describes the miraculous feeding of 5,000 people with the five barley loaves and two fish sometime before the Passover. All of the Gospel writers wrote about Yeshua's experience in Jerusalem and the events leading up to the last Passover with the disciples and His final trial and crucifixion.

John 7 describes events leading up to and what transpired at the Feast of Tabernacles. At this feast the Jewish scholars marveled at Yeshua's teaching in the temple (John:14-16).

On the last day, that great day of the feast Yeshua [Jesus] *stood and cried out, saying, "If any one thirst, let him come to Me and drink. He who believes in Me as the Scriptures has said, out of his heart will flow rivers of living water."* (John 7:37, 38).

The Bible declared that the following morning, Then Yeshua [Jesus] spoke to them again, saying, *"I am the light of the world. He who follows Me shall not walk in darkness, but have the light of life"* (John 8:12). Yeshua, the Messiah, said that if anyone thirsts, let him come. He came that all mankind who hear His voice and obey will no longer have to walk in darkness.

CHAPTER NINE

WHY THE SABBATH
SHOULD BE OBSERVED

A great proportion of Gentile or nation believers and Christians are under the notion that Sunday is the Sabbath day while others believe that one can choose any day of the seven days of the week to observe as the Sabbath. Many others are completely unaware that the Sabbath, an appointed day of rest, exists for all believers. In addition, some do not believe the Sabbath is important. However, it is iniquitous to think so because overwhelming evidence in the Bible points to the seventh day of the week, which is Saturday as the Sabbath Day. The following reasons exemplify the importance of observing the Sabbath:

1.   The Sabbath honors and reveres God as our Creator (Genesis 2:2).

2.   The Sabbath was one of the first things God blessed and sanctified (Genesis 2:3).

3.   The Sabbath remembers the exodus from Egypt and that God is the source of our salvation or freedom from the bondage of sin (Deuteronomy 5:15).

4.   The Sabbath is the fourth of the Ten Commandments, the longest command that spans three verses and the only commandment that says "remember" (Exodus 20:8-11; Deuteronomy 5:12).

5.   The Sabbath was also listed on the covenant of testimony given to Moses (Exodus 34:10).

6.   The Sabbath was observed by Yeshua and His disciples (Mark 1:21; 6:2; Luke 4:16; John 8:12; John 15:10).

7.   The Apostle Paul observed the Sabbath (Acts 13:13, 14, 42-44; Acts 17:1, 2; Acts 18:1, 4, 9, 11).

8.   The Sabbath allows the Gentile nations to identify with the Jewish, Hebrew or Israelite people. Understanding and observing the Sabbath will make you a more effective witness to the lost sheep of the house of Israel (Matthew 10:6; 15:24; Jeremiah 50:6).

9.   The Sabbath is a time for celebrating your personal and spiritual rest in our Messiah (Hebrews 4:9, 10).

10.   Observing the Sabbath brings blessings not only to the Jews, Hebrews or Israelites but also to Gentiles or foreigners (Isaiah 56:3-8).

11.   The Sabbath will be honored in the future kingdom of God (Isaiah 66:23).

12.   The Sabbath is a delight and not a burden (John 5:3).

13.   It is a holy day which is honorable to the Lord (Isaiah 58:13, 14).

14.   Observing and honoring the Sabbath is an act of Love and obedience to God (Exodus 20:1-10).

15.   The Sabbath is a perpetual or an everlasting covenant (Exodus 31:16).

The Sabbath, which is not about a church, a denomination, a special ethnicity or a group of people, was purposefully created by God from the beginning of time. It was ordained long before the tabernacle was established as a place of worship. The Sabbath is about the sanctity and holiness of God. It is a designated time period of twenty-four hours, which He carved out for us to rest from the six days of toil and busyness. *Sabbath* not only means "to rest" but also means "to desist, cease, and celebrate." It is a time to forget about the activities of the world and connect with God uninterrupted through worship, praise, Bible study, enjoying the beauty of His creation and finally to be refreshed and to replenish your soul.

> *The Sabbath is* holy by the grace of God, and is still in need of all the holiness which man may lend to it. The Sabbath is meaningful to God, for without it there would be no holiness in our world of time. It is God who sanctified the seventh day. It is a reminder that God is our Father. The Sabbath is all Holiness.[1]

Some additional Scriptures reveal conversations by David, Yeshua, Paul and others which reinforce the need to observe the Sabbath and to obey God's laws.

In Psalm 19:7, 8, David declared:

> "*The law of the* LORD *is perfect converting the soul: the testimony of the* LORD *is sure making wise the simple. The statutes of the* LORD *are right, rejoicing the heart; the com mandments of the* LORD *are pure, enlightening the eyes.*"

In Psalm 25:10 and 14, David continued:

> "*All the paths of the* LORD *are mercy and truth unto such as keep his covenant and his testimonies.* 14*The secret of the* LORD *is with them that fear Him and He will show them His covenant.*"

Psalm 111:7, 8

"The works of His hands are verity and judgment; all His commandments are sure. They stand fast forever and ever and are done in truth and uprightness."

Psalm 111:10

"The fear of the LORD is the beginning of wisdom a good understanding have all they that do His commandments."

Psalm 119:165, 166

"Great peace have those who love your law; And nothing causes them to stumble. LORD, I hope for your salvation, and I do your commandments."

Psalm 119:172

"My tongue shall speak your word, for all your commandments are righteousness."

Matthew 19:16-22 disclosed Yeshua's (Jesus') conversation with the rich young ruler. He asked Yeshua:

"...Good Master, what good thing shall I do, that I may have eternal life? [17]And he said unto him, why callest thou me good? there is none good but one, that is, God; but if thou wilt enter into life, keep the commandments. [18]He saith unto him, Which? Jesus said, Thou shalt do no murder, Thou shalt not commit adultery, Thou shalt not steal, Thou shalt not bear false witness, [19]Honour thy father and thy mother: and, Thou shall love thy neighbour as thyself."

Interestingly, Yeshua refers only to the last six commandments that address relationships with each other. Previously I wondered why Yeshua did not talk about the first four commandments, which are all about loving God as well as including the seventh-day Sabbath observance. I once thought that it was a good reason not to observe the Sabbath.

I later realized that Yeshua did not mention the first four commandments because His Jewish audience knew the law, and they did not have a problem with the first four commandments which relate to loving God. The real problem was with the last six commandments which address dealing with people or relationships with others. This brings to mind the golden rule, *"...do unto others as you would like them do unto you"* (Matthew 7:12; Luke 6:31).

In Matthew 22:36-40, a lawyer (scribe) who was a member of the Sanhedrin asked Yeshua which was the greatest commandment in the law. Yeshua answered:

> *"...Thou shalt love the Lord thy God with all thy heart, and with all thy soul, and with all thy mind. *38*This is the first and great commandment* [See Deuteronomy 6:5]. *39*And the second is like unto it, Thou shalt love thy neighbour as thyself* [See Leviticus 19:18]. *40*On these two commandments hang all the law and the prophets"* (KJV).

A similar discourse is found in Luke 10:25-37 in the parable of the Good Samaritan. A lawyer asked Yeshua:

> *"...Master, what shall I do to inherit eternal life? *26*Jesus then said to him, "what is written in the law? How readest thou?" *27*The lawyer answered Jesus saying, "Thou shalt love the Lord your God with all thy heart, and with all thy*

soul, and with all thy strength, and with all thy mind; and thy neighbor as thyself" [28]*Jesus said to him, "Thou has answered right ; this do and thou shalt live."*

These two great commandments represent the Ten Commandments. The first four hinge on the first great commandment which represents a believer's love and relationship with God. The other six hinge on the second great commandment which represents a believer's love and relationship with his neighbors or others.

The first commandment states that we should worship the one and only God while the second warns us about the worship of idols. It explicitly states that God is jealous, and for those who hate Him iniquities will be handed to the first through the third and fourth generation. However, He will show mercy to thousands who keep His commandments. The third commandment warns that He will hold us guilty for taking the name of the Lord in vain. The fourth commandment says to remember the Sabbath day to keep it holy, reminding us that it is a special and blessed day. The Sabbath was consecrated from the foundation of the world. However, most of Christendom has forgotten this one, very important commandment as they have chosen to do otherwise.

In Romans 13:8-10, Paul expressed similar sentiments to the Romans as Yeshua had declared to the rich young ruler (Matthew 19:20-22) when He said,

"Owe no man any thing, but to love one another, for he that loveth another hath fulfilled the law. [9]*For this, Thou shalt not commit adultery, Thou shalt not kill, Thou shalt*

not steal, Thou shalt not bear false witness, Thou shall not covet; and if there be any other commandment, it is briefly comprehended in this saying, namely, Thou shalt love thy neighbour as thyself. [10]Love worketh no ill to his neighbor; therefore love is the fulfilling of the law." (KJV)

Paul's letter to the Galatians said, *For all the law is fulfilled in one word, even in this: "You shall love your neighbor as yourself"* (Galatians 5:14). James, the brother of Yeshua, said: *"If you really fulfill the royal law according to the scripture, 'you shall love your neighbor as yourself.' You shall do well."* (James 2:8) An expressive emphasis has been placed on the last six commandments because it is in the area of people relationships that the people were greatly lacking. It is not suggesting that the first four commandments are unimportant.

In John 13:34 Yeshua said to His disciples, *"A new commandment I give to you that you love one another as I have loved you, that you also love one another."* He repeated this command yet again in John 15:12-14:

"This is My commandment, that you love one another as I have loved you. [13]Greater love has no one than this, than to lay down His life for His friends. [14]You are my friends if you do what I command you."

Indeed, love is the central theme in the commandments. Obeying all of God's law and commandments and living by the standards Yeshua, the Messiah, set for us to follow is an expression of our love for God and people. Therefore, God's law demands that we love God more than we love ourselves, and we are to love our neighbor as we love ourselves. Yeshua came, and through His agape love, He satisfied the law by strict obedience to His Father and surrendering His life for us.

> *"For God so loved the world that He gave His only begotten Son, that whoever believes in Him shall not perish but have everlasting life. [17]For God did not send His son into the world to condemn the world, but that the world through Him might be saved"* (John 3:16, 17).

Yeshua came as the sacrificial Lamb for the remission of our sins and to point us to the way of salvation and the standards by which to live in satisfying the requirements for inheriting eternal life. The prophet Isaiah declared that the Lord would magnify the law and make it honorable (Isaiah 42:21).

Yeshua, the Messiah, taught and kept the commandments, and no evidence exists in the Scriptures where He mentioned that we should disobey them as well as teach others to disobey them. The hallmark of the Ten Commandments is love. I John 5:2 (KJV), *"By this we know that we love the children of God, when we love God, and keep his commandments."* Paul stated in I Timothy 1:5 that the purpose of the commandment is love out of a pure heart and of a good conscience and sincere faith. Romans 8:28 is a favorite Scripture for believers: *"And we know that all things work together for good to those who love God, to those who are called according to his purpose."* The question is: do you love God and is His purpose working through you?

In John 14:15, Yeshua said, *"If you love me, keep my commandments."* Surprisingly, it's about 2,000 years since the Messiah came, and a great percentage of the world's population has been taught to keep Sunday as the Sabbath while violating the

Sabbath commandment, the seventh day, which is an indication of our respect and love for God. In verse 21, He further stated:

"He who has my commandments and keeps them, it is he who loves me. And he who loves me will be loved by my Father, and I will love him and manifest myself to him."

It was the customary for Yeshua to observe the Sabbath, and He also went to the temple and taught (Luke 4:16, 31 and Mark 6:2). Instances are recorded of times when He performed acts of mercy. In Mark 6: 6-10, Yeshua healed the man with the withered hand. In Mark 13:10-14, He healed the woman with the infirmity. In Matthew 2:1-8 and Mark 2:23-28, the Pharisees challenged Yeshua because the hungry disciples reaped corn on the Sabbath. In each of these actions, Yeshua showed that it is acceptable to perform deeds of mercy and necessities on the Sabbath. It is not worthy to observe the Sabbath so rigidly that we miss out on the great act of showing kindness to others.

Yeshua declared that the Son of Man was Lord over the Sabbath, and the Sabbath was made for man—not man for the Sabbath. He did not say the Sabbath was reserved for the Jews or Hebrews/Israelites alone. In essence, Yeshua is reminding man that the Sabbath belongs to God. The choice is not for man to decide the day of the Sabbath. Therefore, He has authority over the Sabbath, and He knows what is considered appropriate to do on the Sabbath. When the Sabbath is dishonored, we dishonor God. Leviticus 23:3 clearly states: *"It is the Sabbath of the LORD."* Yeshua is the Creator of all things (John 1:3 and Colossians 1:16), and yet He kept the Sabbath.

Yeshua's sermon on the mount is clearly one of the hallmarks of His teaching and He made this focal statement in His message.

> *"Do not think that I came to destroy the Law or the Prophets. I did not come to destroy but to fulfill. [18]For assuredly, I say to you, till heaven and earth pass away, one jot or tittle will by no means pass from the law till all is fulfilled. [19]Whoever therefore breaks one of the least of these commandments, and teaches men so, shall be called least in the kingdom of heaven; but whoever does and teaches them, he shall be called great in the Kingdom of heaven. [20]For I say unto you unless your righteousness exceed the righteousness of the Pharisees, you will by no means enter the kingdom of Heaven"* (Matthew 5:17-20).

The word *jot* is defined as "the smallest letter in the Hebrew alphabet"—the same as *Iota* in the Greek alphabet which means "the smallest part of anything." A *tittle* is "a small horn-shaped mark similar to an accent, which means a small particle or the least of anything." Luke 16:17 also recorded, *"And it is easier for heaven and earth to pass than one tittle of the law to fail."* Yeshua is explaining how important and significant even that part of the law which one might consider minute or infinitesimal. Yeshua has given us an example as echoed by Him and recorded in John 15:10, which says, *"If you keep my commandments, you will abide in my love just as I have kept my Father's commandments and abide in His love."*

First John 2:3 and 4 states, *"Now by this we know that we know Him if we keep His commandments. He who says, I know Him and does not keep his commandments is a liar, and the truth* is not in him." Verse 6 continues, *"He who says he abides in Him ought himself also to walk just as He walked."*

First John 5:3 adds, *"For this is the love of God, that we keep His commandments. And His commandments are not burden-some."* James, the brother of Yeshua, said, *"For whoever shall keep the whole law and yet stumble in one point he is guilty of all"* (James 2:10).

James, who was also the leader of the Jerusalem Church, met with elders, Paul, Peter and other apostles to discuss matters of the church's including the conflict over circumcision. At the time some of the Jewish, Hebrew, or Israelite-Messianic converts believed that the Gentile converts needed to be circumcised in order to be saved. Subsequent to the meeting of this Jerusalem Council, Barnabas and Silas were dispatched with a letter to the church of Antioch. (See Acts 15.)

Paul, in addressing this issue in his letter to the Corinthians, stated in 1 Corinthians 7:19, *"Circumcision is nothing, and un-circumcision is nothing, but keeping the commandments of God is what matters."* In his letter to the Romans, he included several statements about the law. In Romans 2:11-13 he said:

> *"For there is no respect of persons with God. ¹²For as many as have sinned without the law shall also perish without the law, and as many as have sinned in the law shall be judged in the law. ¹³For not the hearers of the law are just in the sight of God, but doers of the law will be justified."*

Paul also states the following in Romans 3:28-31:

> *"Therefore we conclude that a man is justified by faith apart from the deeds of the law. Or is He the God of the*

Jews only? ²⁹Is He not also the God of the Gentiles? Yes, of the Gentiles also, ³⁰since there is one God who will justify the circumcised by faith and uncircumcised through faith. ³¹Do we then make void the law through faith? Certainly not! On the contrary we establish the law."

Paul's statement is solidifying the fact that the law stands firm regardless of a person's faith.

Paul said in Romans 7:12, *"Therefore the law is holy, and the commandment holy, just and good."* First John 3:4 (KJV) contains the statement, *"Whosoever committeth sin transgresseth also the law; for sin is the transgression of the law."*

The law teaches us what sin is. God's law is a statement of His holiness; therefore, it is of vital importance that we never forget the law—even though we are saved by *grace* or "God's unmerited favor" and not by the works of the law. The law and commandments of God are based on love, trust, truth and obedience. In Matthew 19:17, Yeshua's response to the rich young ruler was that if he wanted to enter life, he should keep the commandments. Similar sentiments can be found in John 5:24, which says,

"Most assuredly, I say to you he who hears my word and believes in Him who sent me has everlasting life, and shall not come into judgment, but has passed from death into life."

Invariably, the assurance of eternal life is dependent upon belief, trust and obedience. In his letter to the Ephesians, the Apostle Paul declared:

"For by grace you have been saved through faith, and that not of yourselves: it is the gift of God. Not of works, lest anyone should boast. For we are his workmanship, created in Yeshua for good works, which God prepared beforehand that we should walk in them" (Ephesians 2:8-10).

How should we walk? Apostle Paul said, *"that you may walk worthy of the Lord fully pleasing Him, being fruitful in every good work and increasing in the knowledge of God"* (Colossians 1:10).

Certainly to walk worthy is believing, trusting, loving God and people and be obedient to His commands as manifested in His words. It is also important to apply this daily in our lives. The Scriptures implore us to walk in faith, in forgiveness, in love, in spirit, in wisdom, in the light, and in truth. Yeshua is the perfect embodiment of all these characteristics. Second John 4 and 6 state:

"I rejoice greatly that I have found some of your children walking in truth, as we received commandment from the Father. ⁶This is love, that we walk according to His commandments. This is the commandment, that as you have heard from the beginning, you should walk in it."

The Sabbath (the fourth commandment) was established as a perpetual covenant (Exodus 31:16). It was not merely for the Jews, Hebrews or Israelites. Gentile believers are to be grafted in and become spiritual Israelites.

For if the first fruit is holy, the lump is also holy: and if the root is holy so are the branches. ¹⁷And if some branches were broken off, and you being a wild olive tree were grafted in among them, and with them become a partaker of the root and fatness of the olive tree, [18]do not boast against the branches. But if you do boast remember that you do not support the root but the root supports you. [19]You will say then, "Branches were broken off that I might be grafted in" (Romans 11:16-19).

As a teenager, I witnessed a horticulturist grafting citrus trees. Dead branches were removed from the tree before grafting. I have seen an orange branch being grafted to a grapefruit tree and a tangerine branch being grafted to an orange tree. I have also seen similar examples of grafting which were already bearing citrus. One observation I made was that each tree still had a single root and trunk even though the branches and fruits varied.

It is very clear that Gentile believers are a part of God's redemptive plan as they have been grafted in; therefore, it is unwise for any believer to think that some parts of the Bible are reserved for the Jews, Hebrews or Israelites alone. Galatians 3:28, 29 says it best:

"There is neither Jew nor Greek, there is neither slave nor free, there is neither male nor female: for you are all one in Yeshua-Messiah. [29]And if you are in Yeshua Messiah, then you are Abraham's seed, and heirs according to the promise."

What was this promise to Abraham?

1) *"In your seed all the nations of the earth shall be blessed, because you have obeyed my voice"* (Genesis 22:18).

2) *"That the Gentiles should be fellow heirs of the same body, and partakers of His promise in Christ through the gospel"* (Ephesians 3:6).

3) *"There shall be a root of Jesse. And He shall rise to reign over the Gentiles, In him the Gentiles have hope"* (Romans 15:12).

In Romans 15:12, Paul was quoting the words of the prophet as stated in Isaiah 11:1 and 10. As Isaiah continued his prophetic message about Yeshua's first coming, he made some bold statements. Isaiah 42:4 (KJV) states, *"He shall not fail nor be discouraged, till he have set judgment in the earth; and the isles* [Gentiles] *shall wait for his law."*

Verse 6 (KJV) continues,

"I the LORD have called thee in righteousness, and will hold thine hand, and will keep thee, and give thee for a covenant of the people, for a light of the Gentiles."

Isaiah went on to make this statement in verse 21: *"The LORD is well pleased for his righteousness' sake; he will magnify the law, and make it honourable"* (KJV).

According to the prophet as reported in Isaiah 49:6,

"And he said, It is a light thing that thou shouldest be my servant to raise up the tribes of Jacob, and to restore the preserved of Israel; I will also give thee for a light to the Gentiles, that thou mayest be my salvation unto the end of the earth." (KJV)

Verse 22 continues:

"Thus saith the LORD God, Behold, I will lift up mine hand to the Gentiles, and set up my standard to the people; and they shall bring thy sons in their arms, and thy daughters shall be carried upon their shoulders" (KJV).

The prophet Jeremiah also discussed God's restoration of Israel as he emphatically stated: *"For I will bring them back into their land which I gave to their fathers"* (Jeremiah 16:15). Jeremiah also continues God's dialogue in Jeremiah 16:19: *O LORD, my strength and my fortress, My refuge in the day of affliction, the Gentiles shall come to You from the ends of the earth and say "surely our fathers have inherited lies, worthlessness and unprofitable things."*

Therefore, the ultimate task or goal of Yeshua, the Messiah, was for the preservation of Israel, to restore the descendants of Jacob, to bring light to the Gentiles (or nations) and to bring salvation to the world. According to Isaiah, Yeshua's mission included increasing the validity of the law as well as giving honor to the law. The preceding Scriptures from Isaiah make it obviously clear that several hundred years before Yeshua, the Messiah, would come, the Gentiles (or nations) were predestined to be a part of God's substantive plan of salvation. The Psalmist said, *"He sent redemption unto his people: he hath commanded his covenant for ever, holy and reverend is his name"* (Psalm 111:9; KJV). It is evident that God designed His eternal plan for Yeshua, the Messiah, to come and set things in order by His teaching and actions and laying down His life for us, showing to the world the way to inherit His kingdom of eternity.

Gentile believers (or nations) who have accepted Yeshua as

the Messiah and have become His followers are now a part of the Israel of God, having been grafted into the "Olive Tree," and as such, have a responsibility to reach out in love and be witnesses to the lost sheep of Israel as well as to the whole world. (See Matthew 10:6, 15, 24, and Jeremiah 50:20). The Messiah fulfilled many of the promises that God made to the forefathers of the Hebrews/Israelites/Jewish people. However, many Jews have not accepted Yeshua as the Messiah, but thankfully, the opportunity for restoration remains available to them.

Interestingly, exactly forty years after Yeshua was crucified, the Romans destroyed the Jerusalem Temple in A.D. 70—thus eliminating the sacrificial system, the method of sacrificing animals and using the blood as the means of seeking atonement for their sins. Therefore, the fact that the old system of reconciliation was done away with and true reconciliation can only be achieved through Yeshua, the Messiah as a result of what He did on the cross at Golgotha was reinforced. This is one law that has been fulfilled.

The rejection of Yeshua as the Messiah by many Jewish people is perhaps partially influenced by the treatment they received throughout the ages in the name of Christianity. They have looked at the sins of the Christian people, have seen how they have consistently violated God's laws, and have thereby mistakenly concluded that the Yeshua whom the Christians follow could not possibly be the Messiah. In reality, the failure or the reluctance of a people to recognize that Yeshua is the Messiah and by refusing to accept Him is a grave misunderstanding. Nevertheless, God has promised to restore the children of Israel.

Paul leaves a reminder in Romans 11:26 and 27, which says:

And all Israel will be saved as it is written; "The deliverer will come out of Zion, And He will turn away the ungodliness from Jacob, ²⁷For this is my covenant with them when I take away their sins."

Also in Isaiah 45:17, it is stated, *"But Israel will be saved in the* LORD *with an everlasting salvation: he shall not be ashamed or confounded world without end."* Malachi the prophet also affirmed that the Elijah will return to help in the reconciliation of the remnants. (See also Revelation 11.)

Matthew 24:1-8 (KJV) reported Yeshua's leaving the temple, and when the disciples tried to show Him the splendor of the buildings, Yeshua objected and said to them, *"...See ye not all these things? verily I say unto you, There shall not be left here one stone upon another, that shall not be thrown down."* (See also Luke 21:5, 6.) Yeshua then went to the Mount of Olives and sat down, and the disciples privately asked Him about the time of His coming and of the end of the world.

"And Yeshua answered and said unto them, Take heed that no one deceive you. ⁵For many shall come in my name, saying, I am Christ; and shall deceive many" (Matthew 24:4, 5).

Yeshua continued His conversation with the disciples and mentioned several warning signs but made it clear that no one would know the hour when He would return. Interestingly, in Matthew 24:20, 21 (KJV), Yeshua said,

"But pray ye that your flight be not in the winter, neither on the sabbath day: ²¹For then shall be great tribulation,

such as was not since the beginning of the world to this time, no, nor ever shall be." (See also Luke 21:20.)

Yeshua's prophetic statement regarding the temple did come to pass with its destruction in A.D. 70 following the Roman invasion and siege of Jerusalem. Many lives were lost during this period of events, and there were massive dispersion of the Jews thereafter. No doubt, Yeshua's statement about the Sabbath is another valid indication of the high significance of the Sabbath.

To be a true believer and follower of Yeshua and to properly serve Him by maintaining a genuine relationship, every believer must live by every word that proceeds out of the mouth of God (Matthew 4:4) and recognize that His Holy Scriptures cannot be broken (John 10:35).

The following statement is also declared in Psalm 89:34, which says, *"My covenant will I not break, nor alter the thing that is gone out of my lips"* (KJV).

CONCLUSION

T he laws and commandments of God found in Tanakh (Old Testament) and reinforced in the B'rit-Chadasha (New Testament) are not about a set of rules and regulations. On the contrary, they are His instructions and guidelines on how to live and maintain a harmonious relationship with Him. Therefore, the instructions of God lay the firm foundation for a moral, ethical and righteous standard for living and helps us to be in covenant with Him. A person's failure to keep God's laws is not simple an act of disobedience; rather, it is also a rejection of God's governance over his life. That failure is also a reflection of adapting to the ways of men who have usurped the authority and sovereignty of God who rules supreme over all.

Is it necessary to keep the commandments? Certainly, yes! In Luke 6: 46, as Yeshua neared the end of his discourse on the sermon on the plains, He made this remark: *"But why do you call me Lord, Lord, and do not do the things which I say?"* John 13:17 says, *"If you know these things, blessed are you if you do them."* Yeshua also uttered a warning about the future end times as recorded in Matthew 24:11, 12, which says, *"Then many false prophets will rise up and deceive many. And because lawlessness will abound the love of many will grow cold."* (See also Matthew 7: 21-23.) Yeshua commanded us to love one another in like manner as He loves us and challenges us in John 15:12, *"if you love me, keep my commandments."* During His last moment with the disciples before His betrayal and arrest while praying to the Father, Yeshua prayed the following for the disciples: *"Sanctify them by your truth. Your word is truth"* (John 17:17). For believers, this is what He said, "I do not pray for these alone [disciples] but also for those [believers] who will believe in me through their [the disciples'] word. And have declared to them your name, and will declare it, that the love with which you loved me may be in them, and I in them." These words are an explicit expression of the depth of Yeshua's love and concern for us.

The Scriptures in the Torah writings and the prophets found in the Tanank (Old Testament) spoke about Yeshua and the reason for His coming. The B'rit-Chadasha (New Testament) writings confirmed what was written about Him and actually showed Yeshua in action.

Yeshua Ha Mashiac came in the order of Melchizedek who was king and priest of Salem. (See Genesis 14:16-18 Psalm 110:4 and Hebrews chapter 7.) Yeshua, the Messiah, fulfilled His priestly role much to the disappointment of many Jews who wanted a king to emancipate them from Roman rule. He fulfilled the spring feast as He was a representation of the Passover lamb, unleavened bread, first fruits and also the promised Comforter (Holy Spirit) which came on the Day of Pentecost/Shavout. On His return, He will fulfill the autumn (fall) feasts.

Significantly, Yeshua's fulfillment of the Passover brought an end to the law of sacrifice. Passover animals are no longer required to be killed and their blood taken by the high priest into the inner chambers of the temple and sprinkled on the mercy

seat which overlaid the ark of the covenant in seeking forgiveness (atonement) for himself and the people. Yeshua became the
ultimate sacrifice once and for all and was crucified on the tree
as the Passover lamb on Passover day A.D. 30. He represents our
redeemer and forgiver of sins. The Bible declared that the veil
of the temple was torn the very moment when He breathed His
last breath, thereby confirming that the blood of sacrificial animals was no longer necessary for the forgiveness of sins. Forty
years later it was reconfirmed with the destruction of the
Jerusalem temple in A.D. 70.

Yeshua's Ascension

Prior to Yeshua's ascension, His last meeting with the disciples is recorded in Matthew 28:18-20, which says:

And Jesus came and spoke to them, saying, "All authority

has been given to Me in heaven and on earth. Go therefore and make disciples of all the nations, baptizing them in the name of the Father and of the Son and of the Holy Spirit. Teaching them to observe all things that I have commanded you: and lo I am with you always even to the end of the age," Amen.

Acts 1:8 declared:

"But he shall receive power after that the Holy Ghost is come upon you and he shall be witnesses to me both in Jerusalem, and in all Judea, and in Samaria and unto the utmost part of the earth."

Every believer has an awesome responsibility to be obedient to God's commands and to be a faithful messenger. God has given every believer the authority to bring the truth of Yeshua to the world. This Truth provides the gift of salvation and the inheritance of eternal life by believing in Yeshua, repenting and accepting him as Savior. Believers also need to obey all of God's laws and commandments. Yeshua said, *"...observe all things I have commanded you."* He did not say *some* things.

Yeshua made it very clear. He did not say we were free to make changes to His statutes, laws and commandments. Yeshua kept the Sabbath, and He did not change the Sabbath to Sunday prior to His ascension, and no evidence exists in the Scriptures to suggest that change. I would like to reiterate what Yeshua said to the Jews with whom He had a serious dialogue when He healed the sick man on the Sabbath and also because He referred to God as His Father.

———◆———

"For if you believed Moses, you would believe me; for he wrote about me. "But if you do not believe his writings, how will you believe my word" (John 5:46).

Then Yeshua said to those Jews who believed Him, "If you abide in my word you are my disciples indeed, and you shall know the truth and the truth shall make you free" (John 8:31-32).

In verse 48, Yeshua continued, *"He who is of God hears God's words therefore you do not hear, because you are not of God."* The Apostle Paul declared in 1 Corinthians 11:1, *"Imitate me as I imitate Yeshua."* From the onset of his conversion, Paul became obedient to the truth and laws of God—teaching, writing, spreading the Gospel, and winning souls for God's kingdom. In his defense before Felix the governor of the province of Judea, Paul said,

"But this I confess to you, that according to the way which they call a sect, so I worship the God of my fathers, believing all things which are written in the law and in the prophets" (Acts 24:12).

Paul reaffirmed the fact that he was a Pharisee, and it is well-known that they upheld the law. Paul also studied under Gamaliel, the famous teacher of the law (Philippians 3:5, Acts 22:33). Luke, who is often described as Paul's physician and the writer of the book of Acts, also made it clear in Acts 25:8 that Paul said nothing against the law. Therefore, it is ridiculous to think that Paul did not adhere to the laws or that he only observed the seventh-day Sabbath to appease the Jews and also worshipped on Sunday. Furthermore, Sunday worship did not surface until many years after Paul's death.

John, whose vision on the Isle of Patmos is a testimony to the churches as written in Revelation 22:12-14, declared.

> "And behold I am coming quickly and My reward is with Me to give to everyone according to his work. "I am Alpha, and Omega, the beginning and the end, the first and the last. Blessed are those who do His commandments that they may have the right to the tree of life, and may enter through the gates into the city."

Yeshua also tells us,

> "Enter by the narrow gate, for wide is the gate and broad is the way that leads to destruction, and there are many who go in by it. ¹⁴Because narrow is the gate and difficult is the way which leads to life, and there are few who find it" (Matthew 7:13, 14; NKJV).

And also written in John 5:24,

> "Most assuredly I say to you he who hears my word and believes in him who sent me has everlasting life and shall not come into judgment but has passed from death into life."

The purpose of the laws and commandments is to establish a standard for obedience and living and to keep us in the right relationship with Yeshua, our Savior. It also helps us to focus and make Yeshua the center of our life. John 3:17 says, "For God did not sent His son into the world to condemn the world but that *the world through Him might be saved."* Importantly, Yeshua came to save the world (people)—not to condemn it. Then what is it that condemns man? Well, it is about the size of a person's fist, pounding below our left breast—our heart! Yeshua renewed the covenant through the ratification of His blood and giving access to His being the propitiator for our sins. As promised, the covenanted words would be written on our hearts following the circumcision (conversion) and the indwelling of the Holy Spirit. It is the heart that convicts us to act according to our free will to obey or disobey. A check of the Bible reveals several verses about the heart, and if you were to read only one verse each day, it would take several months to complete.

Some of the Scriptures mentioned about the heart include the following:

David's heart condemns him (2 Samuel 24:10).
- *"For as he thinks in his heart so is he"* (Proverbs 23:17).
- *"My heart also instructs me"* (Psalm 16:7).
- *"For he knows the secret of the heart"* (Psalm 44:21).
- *"For the LORD searches all hearts and understands all the intent of the thoughts"* (2 Chronicles 28:9).
- *"Apply your heart to instruction and your ears to the words of knowledge"* (Proverbs 23:12).
- *"With the heart one believes unto righteousness"* (Romans 10:10).
- *"Beloved, if our heart does not condemn us we have confidence toward God. And whatever we ask we receive from him because we keep his commandments and do those things that are pleasing in his sight"* (1 John 3:21, 22).

The wise King **Solomon** wrote:
- *"Let us hear the conclusion of the whole matter, Fear God and keep His commandments, for this is the whole duty of man. For God will bring every work into judgment, including every secret thing, whether good or evil"* (Ecclesiastes 12:13, 14).

John the disciple declared:
- *"But whoever keeps His word truly the love of God is perfected in him"* (1 John 2:5).

Ten days after Yeshua's ascension, the day of Pentecost/ Shavout, the Ruach Hakodesh, or the Holy Spirit empowered the disciples and several others who were assembled in Jerusalem. Three thousand souls were saved and believed in the Messiah and ushered in the Messianic era. The church evolved, and for the next forty years, the church expanded to the Mediterranean regions, incorporating both Jews and Gentile believers. The assassination of the disciples disquieted the movement, and by the second century, changes began with Sunday worship and later rebranding as Christianity.

A century later Constantine the emperor of the Roman Empire and the religious leaders formulated the tenets of Christianity and made changes regarding the Sabbath and holy feast days (God's appointments with His people), disconnected from the ways established by God and then regarded them as Jewish customs. In doing so, they infused many pagan rituals which are still evident in many Christian churches. The days, time, and names which man has changed and substituted in contradiction to the biblical truths seem to align with these words interpreted

Conclusion

————◆————

from Daniel's vision, *"he shall speak pompous words against the most high and shall intend to change times and law"* (Daniel 7:25; NKJV).

Significantly, many Jews still have not accepted Yeshua as the Messiah and the prior experience of their forbearers during the past centuries even at the hand of Christianity has made it even more difficult. However Paul said all Israel will be saved (Romans 11:26). The good news, however, is that the Messianic movement, a representation of the first-century church, has been revived. Jewish Rabbis and other teachers are leading many congregations comprised of Jews and or Gentiles in the United States and other parts of the world. The Holy Spirit is and will continue to reveal the truth to many people who are a part of the generation known Biblically as the *"repairers of the breach."* (See Isaiah 58:12.) There is only One God (Elohim) who sent Yeshua to declare the truth and to be the Savior of mankind. Therefore, the standards are one and the same in spite of the controversies, disputings, doctrines and selfish acts which emanated in the past and are still occurring. It is now time to reconnect or make the connection as God lovingly desires.

The Bible is the inerrant living Word of God. It is the final and ultimate authority on all issues concerning to God and His ways. It represents the past, present, and future and is also the directional compass and manual for our lives. The Bible is complete and is comprised of the Old and New Testament (Tanakh and B'rit Chadasha) where there is a great connectivity, and it is continuously vibrant and alive.

I believe every word, and as the writer of Psalm 119 said in verse 160: *"The entirety of your word is truth, and everyone of your righteous judgment endures forever,"* and as the Apostle Peter states, *"But the word of the Lord stands forever"* (I Peter 1:25). God's laws have not changed and will not change. The weekly seventh-day Sabbath and the spring and autumn (fall) feasts, which were ordained by God, are special appointments (set aside) for all believers or followers to celebrate and spend time with Him. They are everlasting covenants. *"Yeshua is the same, yesterday, today, and forever"* (Hebrews 13:8.) His truth should never be compromised. He and the Father are one (John 10:30).

It is my fervent hope that the contents of this book will stimulate a conversation between individuals (Jews and Gentiles) and enable them to recognize the disconnection that exist between both groups of people in relation to the one true and eternal living God (Elohim). The wall of separation has been torn down, having been set in motion with Peter's vision (see Acts 10:9-16) during the time of his reluctancy to take the message of the Gospel to the Gentiles. (See also Ephesians 2:14.) The apostle Paul declared in Romans 11:11-25 that he had a responsibility to provoke the Jews to jealousy and likewise the Gentile believers who have been grafted into the "olive tree," making Jewish and Gentile believers or followers one in the body of the Messiah or the house of Israel, His future Kingdom. (See also Galatians 3:28, 29.)

It is prudent, my friend, that you read, study, make the connection, and let God the Father, Yeshua, the Messiah, through the Holy Spirit guide you as you decide for yourself how to love, honor, worship, serve, truly obey, and glorify Him today and in preparation to be a part of His future eternal kingdom. The

Psalmist says, *"Show me thy ways, O Lord, teach me thy paths. Lead me in thy truth and teach me. For thou art the God of my salvation* (Psalm 25:3, 4).

Finally, if you have not accepted Yeshua, the Messiah, or do not believe in Him as your Sovereign leader and Savior of your life, call out to Him; the opportunity is available to you today. Yeshua said, *"he who believes and is baptized will be saved"* (Mark 16:16). The Bible also states *"that if thou shalt confess with thy mouth the Lord Jesus* [Yeshua], *and shalt believe in thine heart that God hath raised him from the dead, thou shalt be saved"* (Romans 10:9). A believer is saved by grace through faith or trust in Yeshua and sanctified by His truth. Yeshua said, *"I am the way the truth and the life, no man comes to the Father but by me"* (John 4:16). God's truth is permanent, unchanging, and everlasting.

Love and Peace.

ENDNOTES

CHAPTER THREE

[1]James Porter, *The Sabbaths of God: The Meaning of God's Holy Days to Christians* (New York: Exposition Press, 1966), 325.

CHAPTER FIVE

[1]Ray Comfort, *The Way of the Master* (Alachua, Fla.: Bridge-Logos Publishers, 2006).

[2]*New Encyclopedia Britannica*, 15th edition, s.v. "Saint Justin Martyr," Chicago: Encyclopedia Britannica, 1992.

[3]Given the 7th of March, Crispus and Constantine being Consuls each of them the second time, Codex Justianus, lib 3, tit. 12.3; translated by Philip Schaaf, D.D., *The History of the Christian Church* (8 vol.) Vol. 3 (New York: Hendrickson Publishers, Inc., 1884), 380 (www.SundayLaw.net).

[4]Newadvent.org; Wikipedia.org; relunctantmessenger.com.

[5]Dr. Samuele Bacchiocchi, "How Did Church on Sunday Begin?" Livingtheway.org.

[6]"Faith of Our Fathers," 1877, p. 108.

[7]*Catholic Mirror*, official organ of Cardinal Gibbons, September 23, 1893.

[8]Stephen Keenan, *A Doctrinal Catechism: Catholic Faith and Practice* 3rd ed., (New York: Edward Dunigan and Brother, 1848), 174.

[9]"Papa,"Translated from Lucius Ferraris, *Prompta Biblio-theca* (Ready Library), article 2.

[10]*Catholic Mirror*, 2 September 1893.

[11]Personal correspondence, Albert Smith, chancellor of the Archdiocese of Baltimore, replying for the Cardinal in a letter of 10 February 1920.

[12]N. Summerfield, *History of the Christian Church*, 1873, p. 415.

[13]The Catholic Virginia, 3 October 1947, p. 9.

[14]Personal Correspondence, Cardinal Gibbons, 1906

[15]Peter Geiermann, C.S.S.R., The Converts Catechism of Catholic Doctrine, 1957, p. 50.

[16]T. Enright, Unpublished Lecture Notes, Hartford, Kansas, February, 1844.

[17]*The Catholic Universal Bulletin*, 14 August 1942, p. 4.

[18]Andrew Nugent Dugger, *A History of the True Religion: From 33 A.D. to Date* (Pub. by A. N. Dugger and C. O. Dodd, 1972) 196-97.

[19]*The Sunday Problem*, a study book of the United Lutheran Church, 1923, p. 36.

[20]Martin Luther, "Augsburg Confession of Faith," Art. 28, 1530, as published in *The Book of Concord of the Evangelical Lutheran Church* edited by Henry Jacobs, 1911, p. 63.

[21]John Theodore Mueller, Sabbath or Sunday, 15-16, Excerpt from "Roman Catholic and Protestant Confessions About Sunday," http://eliyah.com/admit.htm.

[22]Dr. Augustus Neander, *The History of Christian Religion and Church During the First Three Centuries*, Translated by Henry John Rose, 1843, p. 186.

Endnotes

[23]Isaac Williams, *Plain Sermons, on the Latter Part of the Catechism*, Vol. 1 (London: Francis and John Rivington, 1851), 334, 336.

[24]Bishop Seymour, "Why We Keep Sunday," Excerpt from "Roman Catholic and Protestant Confessions About Sunday."

[25]Canon Eyton, "The Ten Commandments," pp. 52, 63, 65, Excerpt from "Roman Catholic and Protestant Confessions About Sunday," http://www.biblesabbath.org/confessions.html

[26]Phillip Carrington as quoted in *Toronto Daily Star*, 26 October 1949.

[27]John Wesley, *The Works of the Rev. John Wesley, A.M.*, John Emory, ed., Sermons 25, Vol. 1 (New York: Eaton & Mains, 1831) 221.

[28]Harris Franklin Rall, *Christian Advocate*, 2 July 1942, p. 26.]

[29]D. L. Moody, *Weighed and Wanting* (New York: Fleming H Revell, Co.) pp. 47-48.]

[30]D. L. Moody speaking at San Francisco, 1 January 1881.

[31]T. C. Blake, D.D., *Theology Condensed*, pp. 474-75, Except from "Historic Denominational Statements on the Sabbath," http://www.sabbathtruth.com/sabbath-history/denominational-statements-on-the-sabbath/id/993/presbyterian.

[32]T. M. Morer, *Dialogues on the Lord's Day*, Except from "Historic Denominational Statements on the Sabbath."

[33]Dr. Edward T. Hiscox, as reported in *New York Examiner*, 16 November 1893.

[34]Alexander Campbell, *The Christian Baptist*, 2 February 1824, Vol. 1. No. 7, p. 164.

[35]"First Day Observance," pp. 17, 19.

[36]Dr. R. W. Dale, *The Ten Commandments* (New York: Eaton & Mains, 1884) 127-29.

[37]Joseph Bingham, *Antiquities of the Christian Church*, Vol. 11, Book xx, Chap 3, Sec 1, 66.1137-38.

[38]John Trigilio, PhD., and Kenneth Brighenti, PhD., *Catholicism for Dummies* (Hoboken, N.J.: For Dummies, 2012.

CHAPTER SIX

[1]*Encyclopedia Britannica*, 11th edition, s.v. "Sunday," Chicago: Encyclopedia Britannica, 1992.

[2]"First Council of Nicaea," Wikipedia Free Encyclopedia.

[3]T. Alton Bryant, *The Compact Bible Dictionary* (Grand Rapids: Zondervan, 1967).

[4]Encyclopedia Britannica, vol. 3, 15th ed., p. 282.]

[5]*The Compact Bible Dictionary*, 370.

[6]A. Jan Marcussen, "National Sunday Law," 1983, p. 90.

CHAPTER EIGHT

[1]James Porter, *The Sabbaths of God: The Meaning of God's Holy Days to Christians* (Hicksville, N.Y.: Exposition Press, 1966.

CHAPTER NINE

[1]Abraham Joshua Heschel, *The Sabbath* (New York: Farrar, Straus and Giroux, 2005) 54, 76, 82.

APPENDIX A
The Names of God*

1. Yahweh/Jehovah—"God Who always is and never changes"
2. Adonai—"God Who is eternal"
3. Elohim—"The majestic God Who is worthy of worship"
4. Jehovah-Elyon—"God most high"
5. El Shaddai—"The Almighty God"
6. Jehovah-Jireh—"God, our Provider"
7. Jehovah-Repheka—"God, our Healer"
8. Jehovah-Tsidkenu—"God, our Righteousness"
9. Jehovah-Nissi—"God, the Conqueror"
10. Jehovah-Shalom—"God, our Peace"
11. Jehovah-Shammah—"The God Who is there"
12. Jehovah-m'Kaddesh—"God Who sanctifies"
13. Jehovah-Ro'eh—"God, our Shepherd"
14. Jehovah-Olam—"God, the everlasting one"

*Victory House, *Prayers That Prevail: The Believer's Manual of Prayers* (Tulsa: Victory House Publishers, 1990).

APPENDIX B
Catholic Catechetical Formula
of the Ten Commandments*

1. "I am the Lord your God. You shall not have strange gods before me."
2. "You shall not take the name of the Lord your God in vain."
3. "Remember to keep holy the Lord's Day."
4. "Honor your father and your mother."
5. "You shall not kill."
6. "You shall not commit adultery."
7. "You shall not steal."
8. "You shall not bear false witness against your neighbor."
9. "You shall not covet your neighbor's wife."
10. "You shall not covet your neighbor's goods."

— — —

*http://www.vatican.va/archive/ccc_css/archive/catechism/command.htm)

APPENDIX C
Hebrew/Jewish
Biblical or Sacred Calendar

T he first month of the biblical sacred calendar begins in the spring shortly before the Passover celebration. These months coincide with two months of the Gregorian or modern-day calendar.

CALENDAR MONTHS	HEBREW NAMES
1. March — April	(Nisan)
2. April — May	(Iyar)
3. May — June	(Sivan)
4. June — July	(Tammuz)
5. July — August	(Av)
6. August — September	(Elul)
7. September — October	(Tishri)
8. October November	(Cheshvan)
9. November — December	(Kislev)
10. December — January	(Tevet)
11. January — February	(Shevet)
12. February — March	(Adar)

APPENDIX D
Hebrew/Jewish Civil Calendar

The Jewish New Year begins on the seventh month Tishri on the Hebrew/Jewish Biblical or Sacred Calender. Therefore, a Jewish year spans across two years on the Gregorian or modern calendar.

CALENDER MONTHS   HEBREW NAME

1. September — October .... (Tishri)
2. October — November .... (Cheshvan)
3. November — December................ (Kislev)
4. December — January................... (Tevet)
5. January — February................... (Shevet)
6. February — March .... (Adar)
7. March — April........................ (Nisan)
8. April — May .... (Iyar)
9. May — June........................... (Sivan)
10. June — July .... (Tammuz)
11. July — August .... (Av)
12. August — September .... (Elul)

SCRIPTURE INDEX

GENESIS 1:31

Genesis 2:2, 3
Genesis 5:24
Genesis 6:7, 8
Genesis 9:11-17
Genesis 10:1-32
Genesis 11:31
Genesis 14:16-18
Genesis 26:5
Genesis 22:18

EXODUS 12:46

Exodus 15:1-21, 26
Exodus 16:4, 5, 11
Exodus 16:17-30, 33, 34
Exodus 19:19, 20
Exodus 20:1-18
Exodus 20-22
Exodus 23:1-12
Exodus 24:5, 7, 8, 12, 15-18
Exodus 31:12-17
Exodus 32:1-6, 19, 25-30
Exodus 33:17-19
Exodus 34:1-4, 6-7, 10-30

Exodus 35:2, 3

LEVITICUS 11

Leviticus 19:18, 30
Leviticus 22:31
Leviticus 23
Leviticus 25:1-8
Leviticus 26:2

NUMBERS 28

Numbers 29

DEUTERONOMY 4:2

Deuteronomy 4:12, 13
Deuteronomy 5:12-15
Deuteronomy 6:4-9, 17
Deuteronomy 8:3, 6, 11
Deuteronomy 12:32
Deuteronomy 14
Deuteronomy 29:1, 9-14
Deuteronomy 30:6

JUDGES 2:11-13

Judges 10:13

I SAMUEL 7:3, 4
I Samuel 12:10
I Samuel 31:10

2 SAMUEL 24:10

I KINGS 9:6-9
I Kings 11:5, 33

2 KINGS 17
2 Kings 23:13
2 Kings 24

I CHRONICLES 9:1

2 CHRONICLES 7:14
2 Chronicles 7:15
2 Chronicles 7:19
2 Chronicles 7:20
2 Chronicles 28:9
2 Chronicles 36:17-21

NEHEMIAH 8:9
Nehemiah 9:1-14
Nehemiah 10
Nehemiah 13:17, 18

PSALM 16:7
Psalm 16:17

Psalm 19:7, 8
Psalm 25:4-5
Psalm 25:10-14
Psalm 44:12
Psalm 81:3-5
Psalm 84:11
Psalm 89:11, 34
Psalm 92
Psalm 95:7, 8
Psalm 103:17, 18
Psalm 110:4
Psalm 111:7-10
Psalm 112:1
Psalm 119:18, 19
Psalm 119:33-35
Psalm 119:86
Psalm 119:142
Psalm 119:151, 155
Psalm 119:160
Psalm 119:165
Psalm 119:166
Psalm 119:172

PROVERBS 3:1
Proverbs 6:23
Proverbs 15:4, 5
Proverbs 23:12, 17
Proverbs 30:5, 6

ECCLESIASTES 12:13, 14

ISAIAH 1:10~20
Isaiah 11:1
Isaiah 29:13
Isaiah 42:8, 21
Isaiah 44:28
Isaiah 45:1-17
Isaiah 48:8
Isaiah 49:6
Isaiah 56:1-8
Isaiah 58:2, 13, 14
Isaiah 66:23

JEREMIAH 11:10, 11
Jeremiah 16: 15, 19
Jeremiah 17:19-27
Jeremiah 31:31-33
Jeremiah 50:6, 20

EZEKIEL 18:4
Ezekiel 20:12
Ezekiel 36:26, 27

DANIEL 7:25

HOSEA 2:11
Hosea 2:14
Hosea 4:6

HABAKKUK 1:5, 6

MALACHI 4:4, 5

MATTHEW 4:4
Matthew 2:1-8
Matthew 5:13, 14
Matthew 5:17-20
Matthew 7:1, 12, 21-23
Matthew 10:6, 15, 24
Matthew 11:28, 29
Matthew 12:12, 40
Matthew 15:9, 24
Matthew 19:16-22
Matthew 22:36-40
Matthew 23:2, 3
Matthew 24:1-8, 11, 12
Matthew 24:20, 22
Matthew 26:17-30
Matthew 27:50-52
Matthew 28:18-20

MARK 1:21, 31, 32
Mark 2:23-28
Mark 6:2, 6-10
Mark 7:5-9
Mark 12:29-31
Mark 13:10-14
Mark 14:12-26

Mark 15:37, 38
Mark 16:1, 2, 9

LUKE 2:42
Luke 4:4, 16
Luke 4:31, 40
Luke 6:5, 31, 46
Luke 10:25-37
Luke 16:17
Luke 17:26, 27
Luke 13:15, 16
Luke 21:5, 6
Luke 21:20, 21
Luke 22:7-20

JOHN 1:1-3, 14
John 1:29
John 2:13-17
John 3:16, 17
John 5:3, 7
John 5:24, 46
John 6:4-14
John 7:37, 38
John 8:12
John 8:31, 32
John 8:48
John 10:22-28
John 10:30, 35
John 12:43-48

John 13:17
John 14:15-17
John 14:34
John 15:10
John 15:12-14, 17
John 17:17
John 19:31, 42
John 20:1, 19

ACTS 1:3, 8, 12, 13
Acts 2:1-4
Acts 2:40
Acts 5:29
Acts 10:9-16
Acts 11:27-30
Acts 13:13, 14
Acts 13:42-44
Acts 14:12-26
Acts 15
Acts 17:1, 2
Acts 20:9-11
Acts 22:3
Acts 18:1, 4, 9, 11
Acts 20:7, 8
Acts 24:12
Acts 25:8

ROMANS 1:5
Romans 2:1-13

Scripture Index

Romans 3:20, 28-31, 37
Romans 4:16
Romans 5:11-13, 20
Romans 6:14, 15
Romans 7:7, 12-25
Romans 8:8
Romans 10:10
Romans 11:16-19, 26, 27
Romans 13:8-10
Romans 14:5, 6, 10-13
Romans 15:12, 25-28
Romans 16:26

I CORINTHIANS 5:7, 8
I Corinthians 7:19
I Corinthians 11:1, 23-30
I Corinthians 15:20, 23
I Corinthians 16:1-4

2 CORINTHIANS 5:10

GALATIANS 2:21
Galatians 3:28, 29
Galatians 5:4, 14

EPHESIANS 2:4
Ephesians 2:8-10
Ephesians 2:11-18
Ephesians 3:6

PHILIPIANS 3:5

COLOSSIANS 1:16
Colossians 2:1-14
Colossians 2:16-18
Colossians 2:20-22

I THESSALONIANS 4:16

2 TIMOTHY 2:15-17
2 Timothy 3:16, 17

HEBREWS 3:15-18
Hebrews 4:1-10
Hebrews 8:1-6
Hebrews 8:7-13
Hebrews 9:1, 10, 15
Hebrews 9:19, 20
Hebrews 9:22-24
Hebrews 10:1-4
Hebrews 10:15-17
Hebrews 11:5
Hebrews 13:8

JAMES 1:25
James 2:10
James 3:6

I PETER 1:25

2 PETER 3:15-18

I JOHN 2:3-6
I John 3:4, 21-22
I John 5:2

2 JOHN 2, 5, 6

JUDE 1:14

REVELATION 1:10
Revelation 4:12, 13
Revelation 11
Revelation 14:12
Revelation 20:6
Revelation 22:12-14, 18-19
Revelation 22:18-19

ABOUT THE AUTHOR

Cleveland C. Anderson retired from the Florida Public School system and is married with two children and one grandchild. He has chosen to write as Lance Caswell because these were the first names he knew as a child. He was called Lance at home, and when he entered elementary school, he was known as Caswell.

He has been a believer most of his life but became a true follower of Yeshua in 1987 when he began paying attention to the messages (Scriptures and sermons), rather than focusing on the messengers (pastors and preachers) as he recognized their imperfections. About fifteen years later, he fully realized that what really matters is one's personal relationship with Yeshua because only that relationship will last and make the difference in how life is lived and allow for a smooth transfer from this earthly life to eternity.

He trusts that you will enjoy reading the information provided in this book, and that it will help you *make the connection*.

www.ingramcontent.com/pod-product-compliance
Lightning Source LLC
LaVergne TN
LVHW051104080426
835508LV00019B/2048